BE WHERE YOU'VE GONE

STUDIES OF THE MALE FIGURE

LAURENCE MORGAN

BE WHERE YOU'VE GONE

STUDIES OF THE MALE FIGURE

LAURENCE MORGAN

Published by the Filbert Press 2021
ISBN 978-1-909054-84-4
Images and text copyright © Laurence Morgan

The Filbert Press is an imprint of

Magic Flute Publishing Limited

231 Swanwick Lane

Southampton SO31 7GT

www.magicflutepublications.co.uk

A catalogue description of this book is available from the British Library

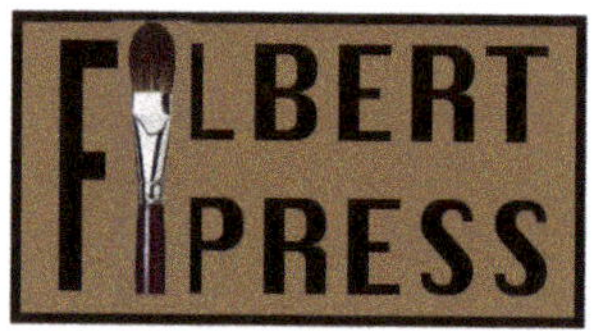

Contents

INTRODUCTION

My journey with art started as a child, going through to my teens with Pottery classes. It consisted less of wheel work but more so free play and within the small group it felt very much like I was adventuring. In 1996 aged twelve I acquired a traumatic brain injury which still impacts me greatly. The focus in recovery was very much learning to use every muscle in my body and communication - initially without speech. I had to learn to solely use my non-dominant hand and arm.

Art was farthest from my mind in my mid twenties when I attended an art group. I needed interaction and to get out of the house. Owing, I believe, to the precision and concentration involved in merely holding a pencil, then the control of marking paper my art quickly progressed and it became "stylised" by the difficulty presented from the quickly fatigued hand and arm and brain. For example creating obstacles to drawing solid lines.

I am untrained, and uncertain of what I intend when I start the process but I will find beauty, or gain intrigue with all my muses. An expression, a pose, an aura! I find beauty in life and people fascinate me. Everyone has a beauty and I love it if I can capture an emotion or wonderful thought.

Laurence Morgan 2021

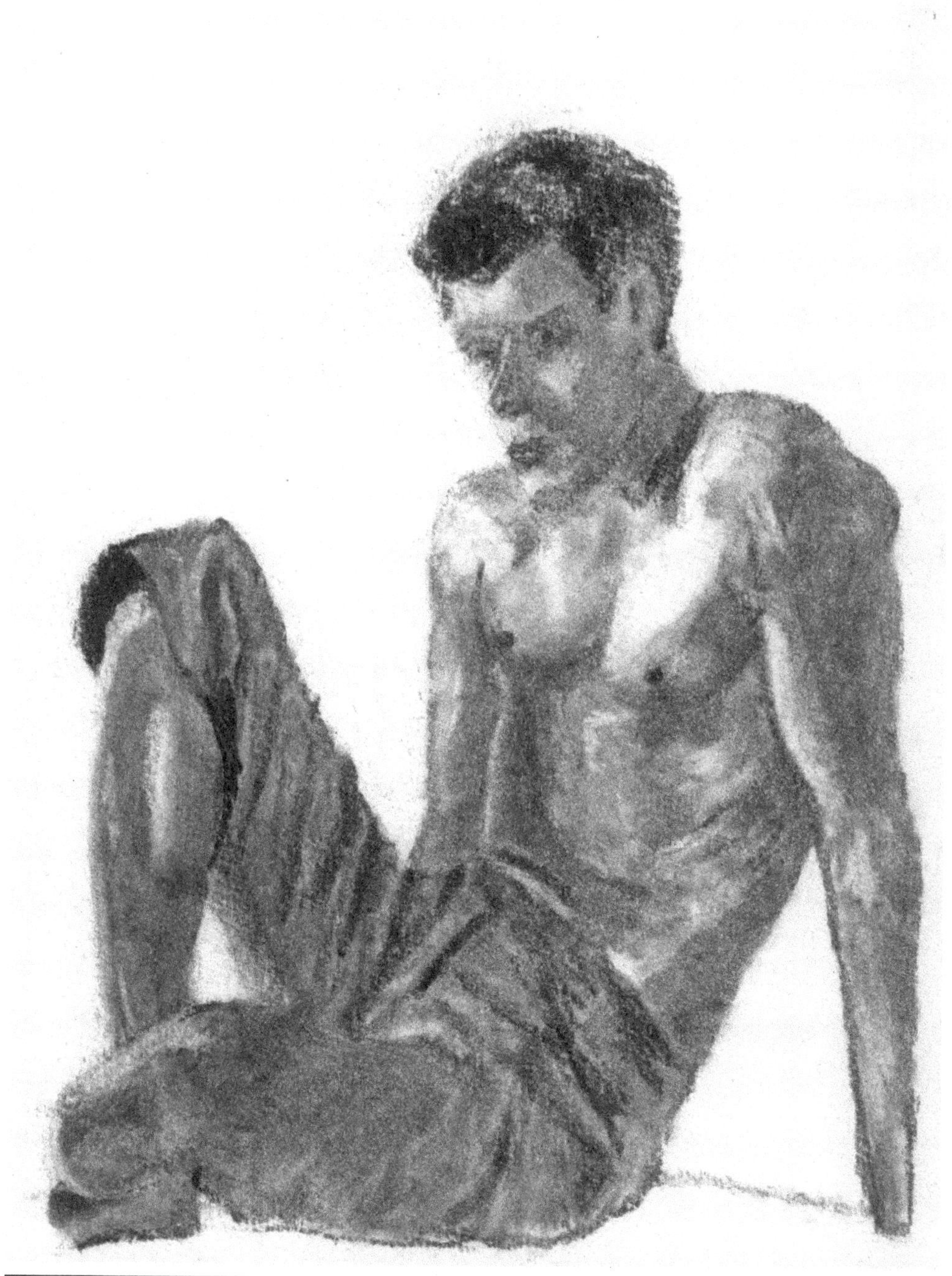

Charcoal Figure
Charcoal on paper. Early 2000.

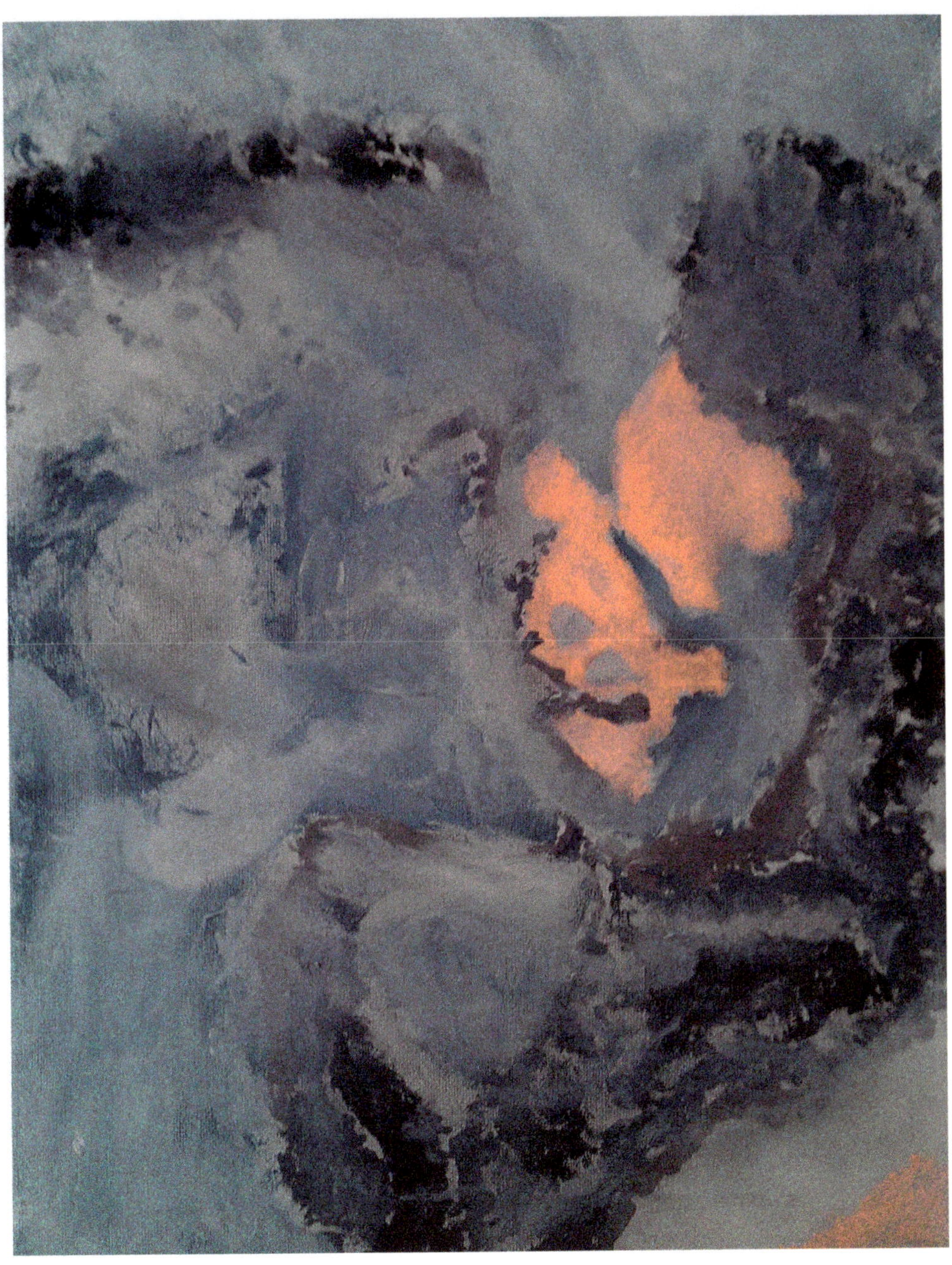

Pervading
Acrylic on canvas. 2011.
An experiment in abstract painting. This piece resides in a private collection.

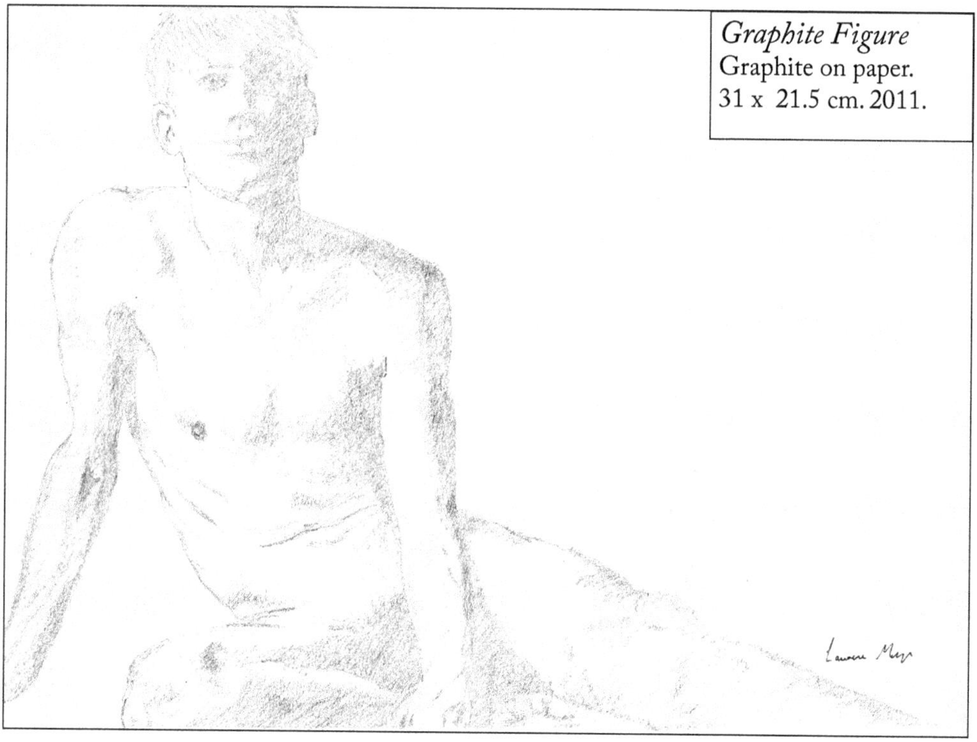

Graphite Figure
Graphite on paper.
31 x 21.5 cm. 2011.

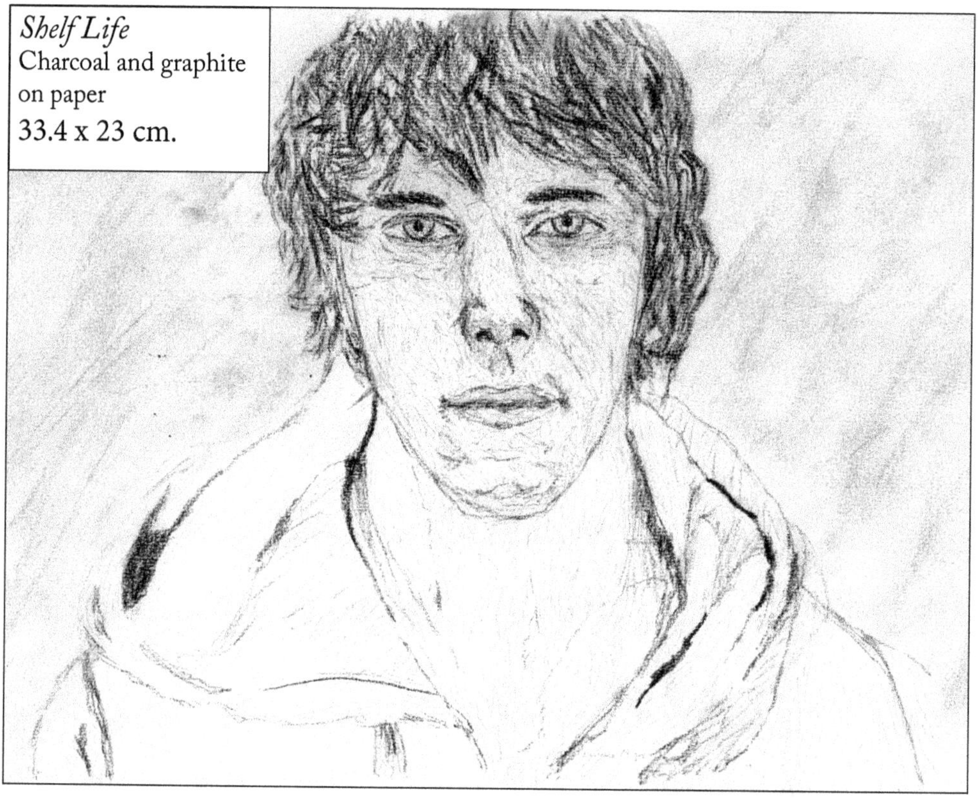

Shelf Life
Charcoal and graphite
on paper
33.4 x 23 cm.

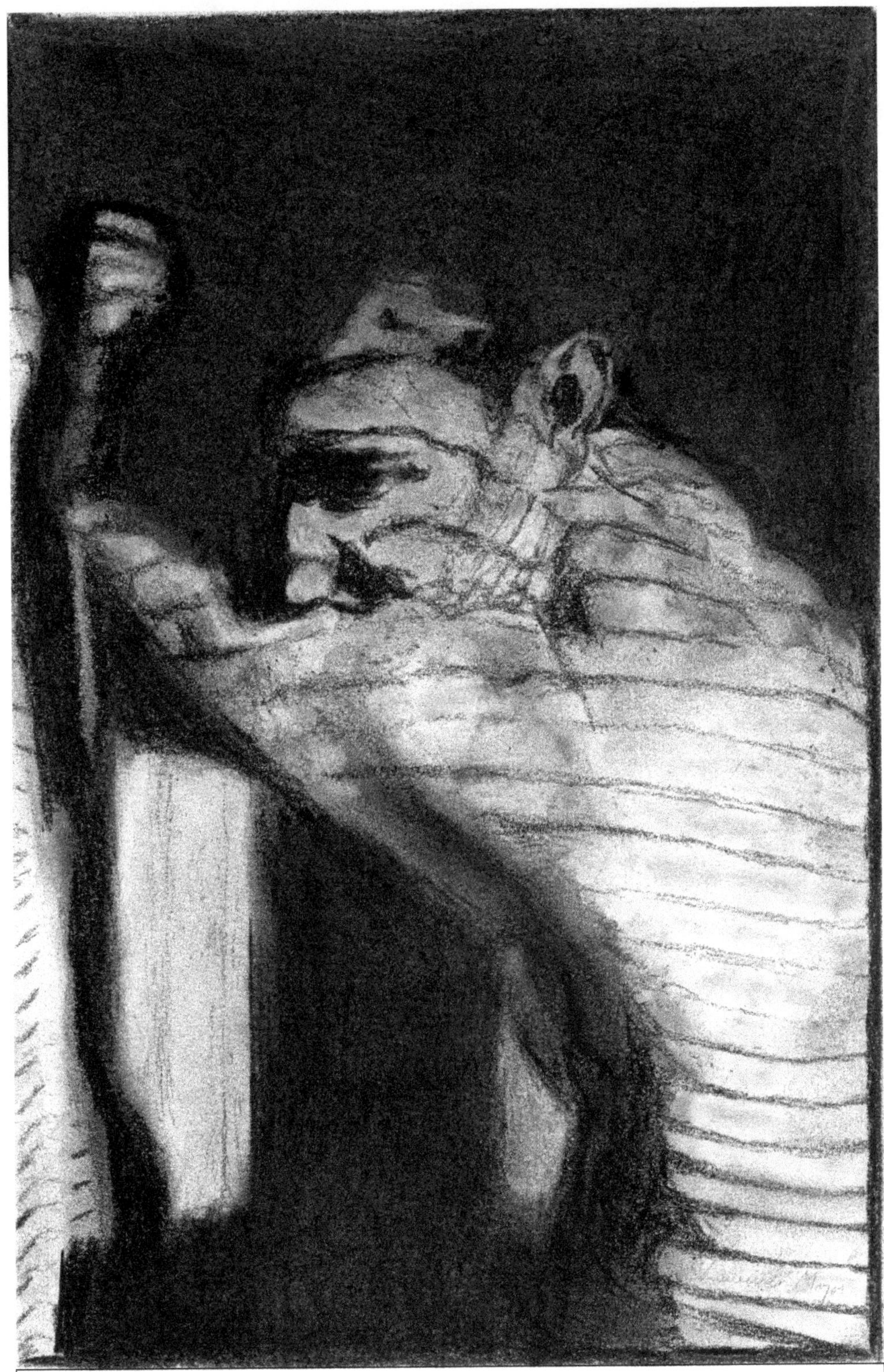

Reflection
Charcoal on paper. This piece resides in a private collection. 2011.

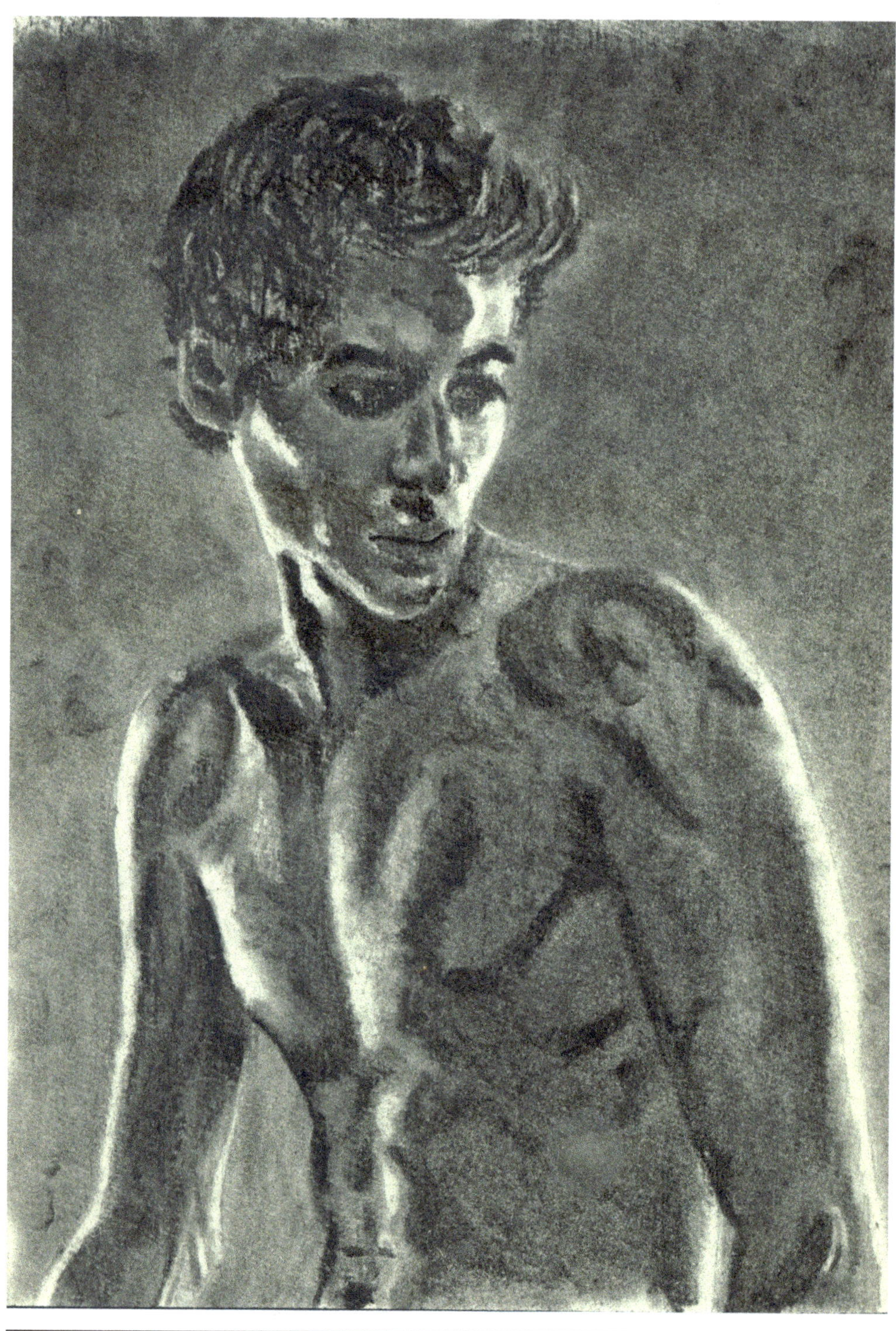

Rapture
Charcoal on paper.

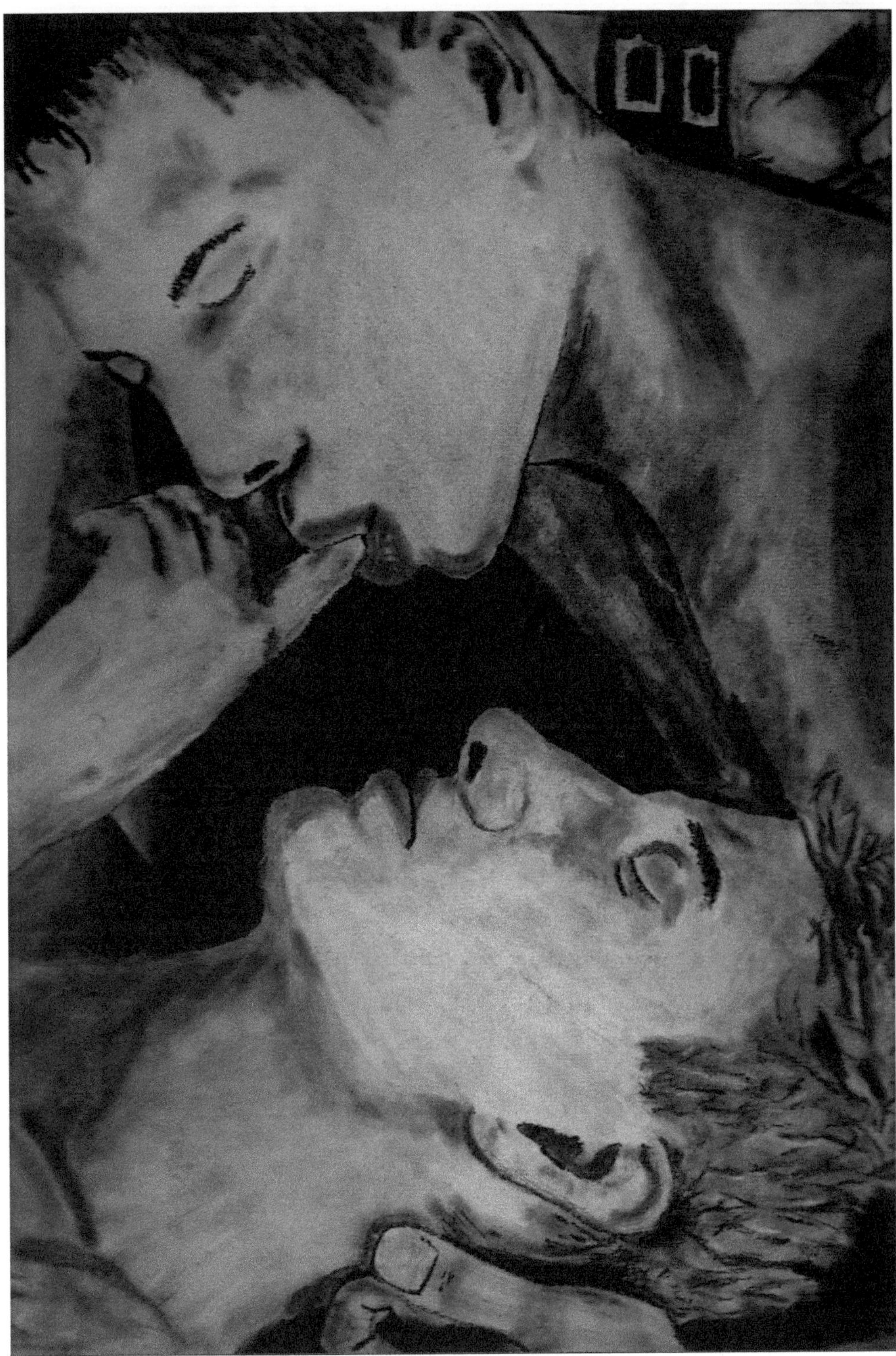

Homeward
Charcoal on paper.
25.2 x 36.9 cm. 2011.

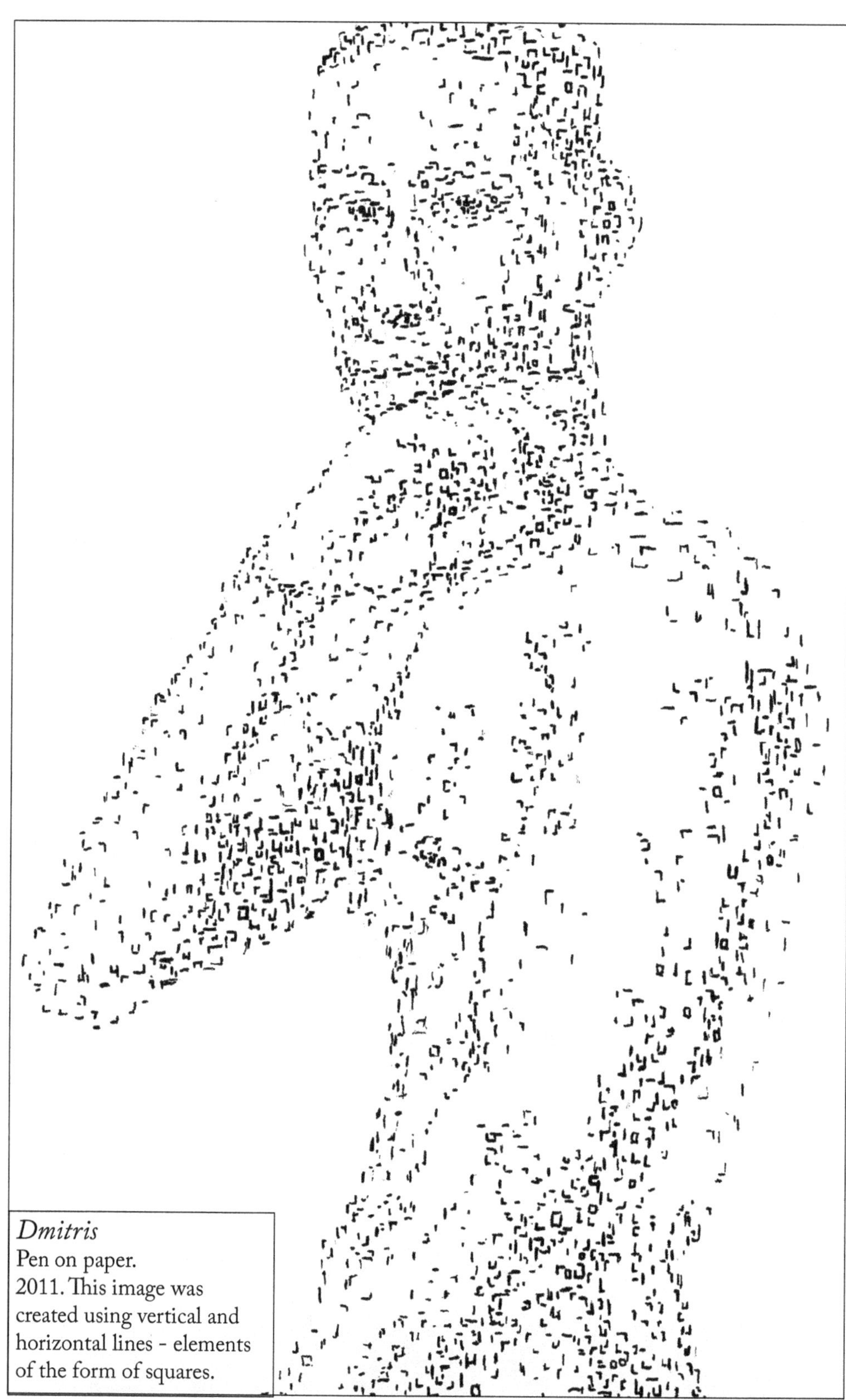

Dmitris
Pen on paper.
2011. This image was
created using vertical and
horizontal lines - elements
of the form of squares.

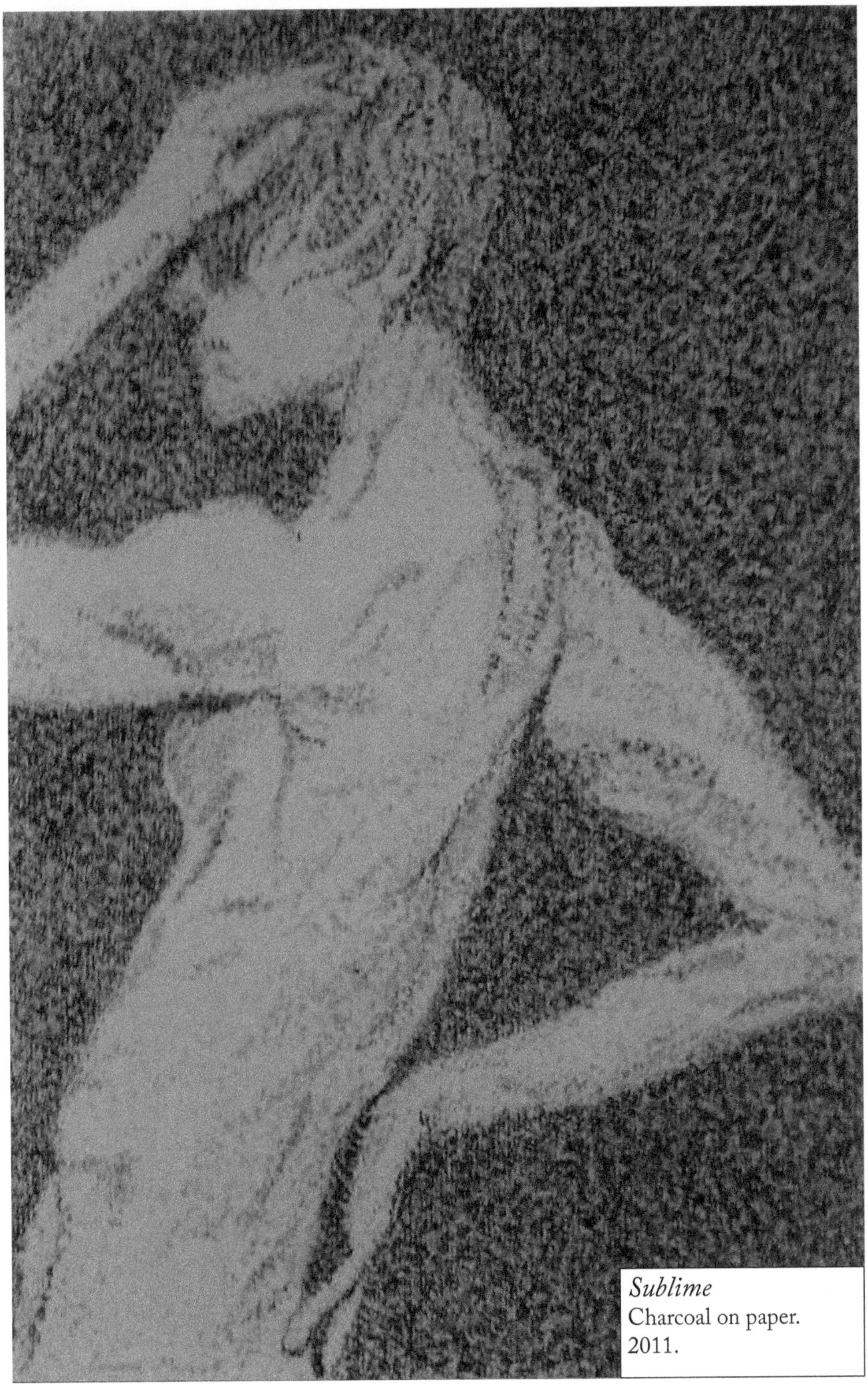

Sublime
Charcoal on paper.
2011.

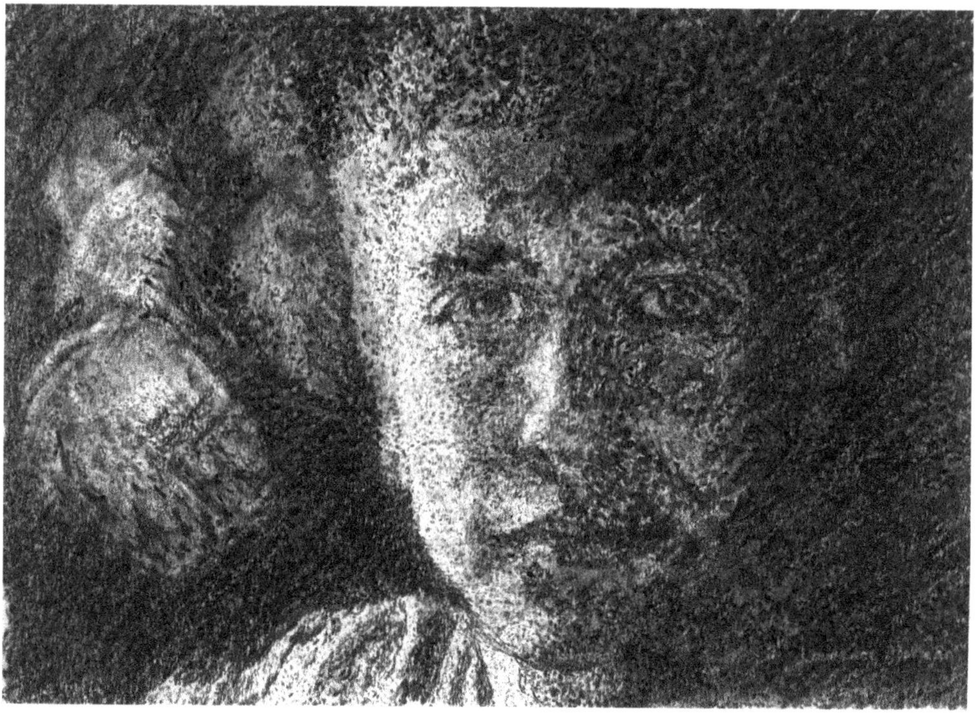

Above:
Chute
Charcoal on paper.
28.5 x 20.5 cm. 2012.
Below:
Conduit
Charcoal on paper. 27.5 x 17 cm. 2012.

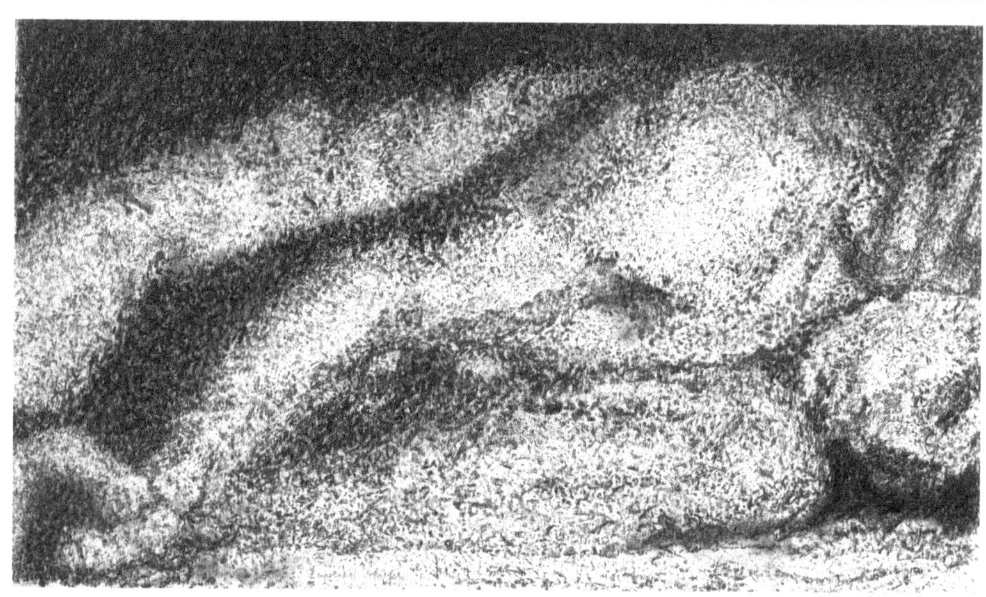

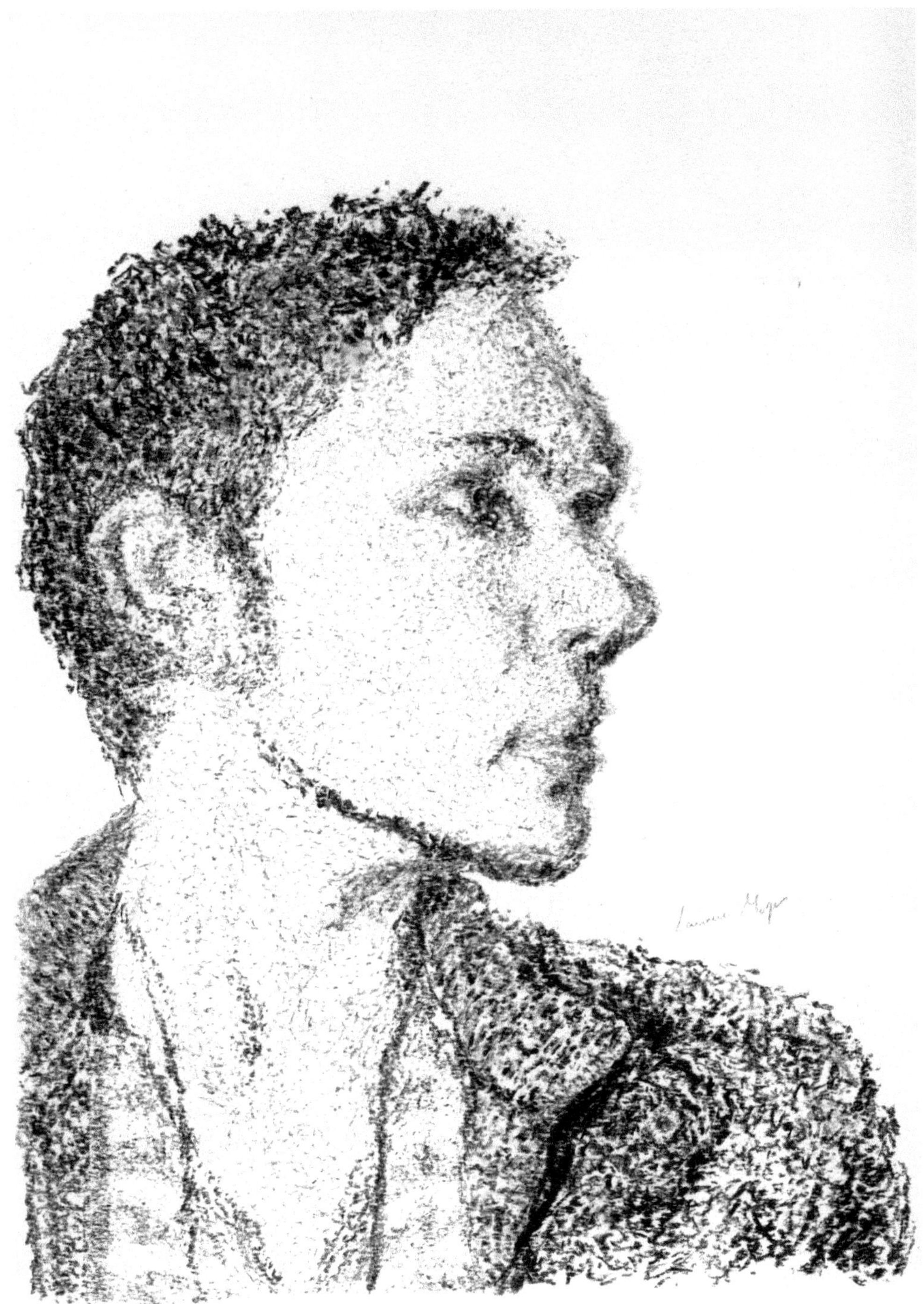

Illuminate
Graphite on paper.
22 x 28 cm.
2012.

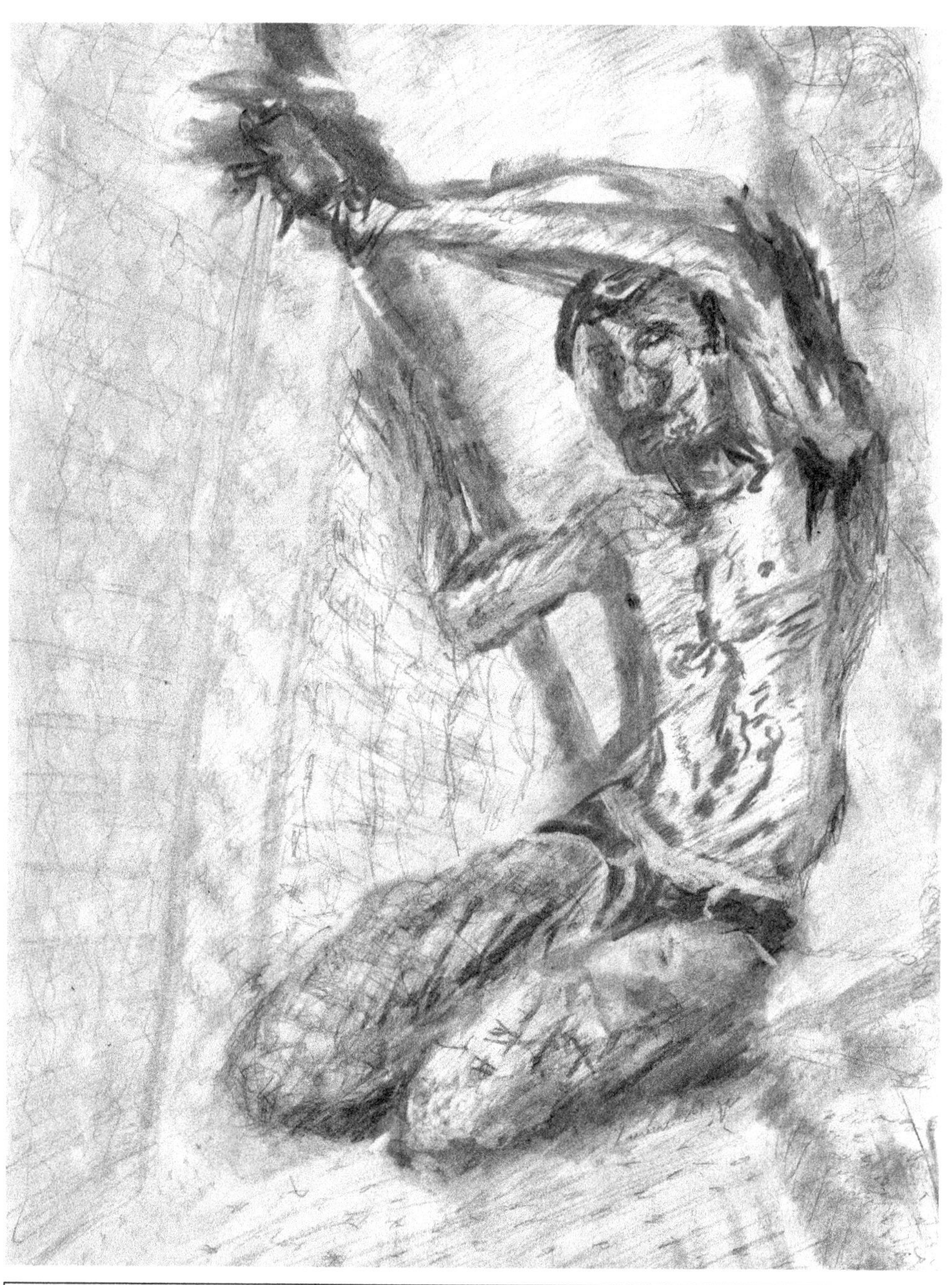

Impaler
Graphite on paper.
48 x 73 cm.
Year 2012.

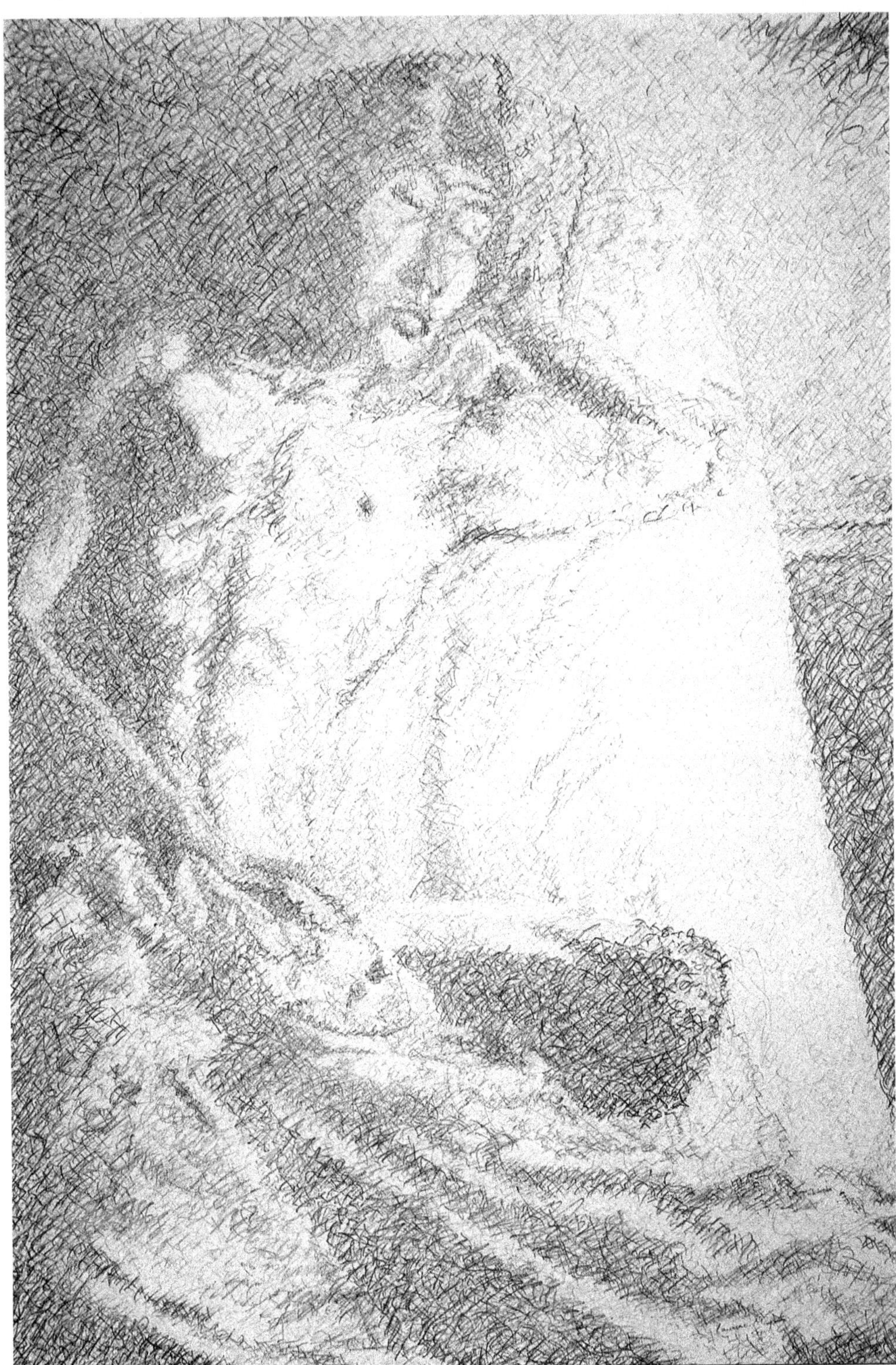

Incubation
Charcoal on paper 52 x 78 cm. 2012.
I made this piece using crosses.

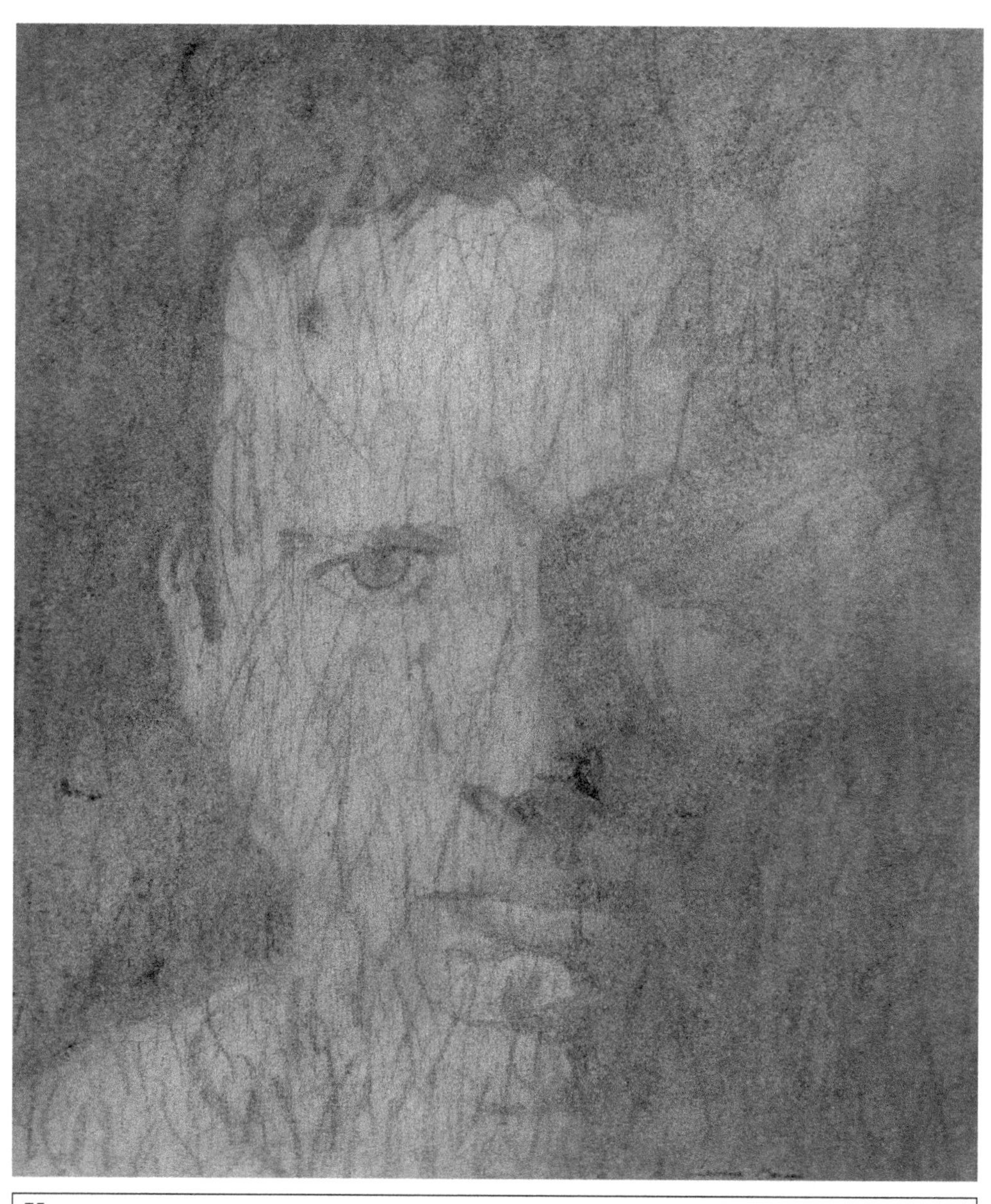

Veneer
Charcoal and spray paint on paper.
27 x 28 cm. 2012.

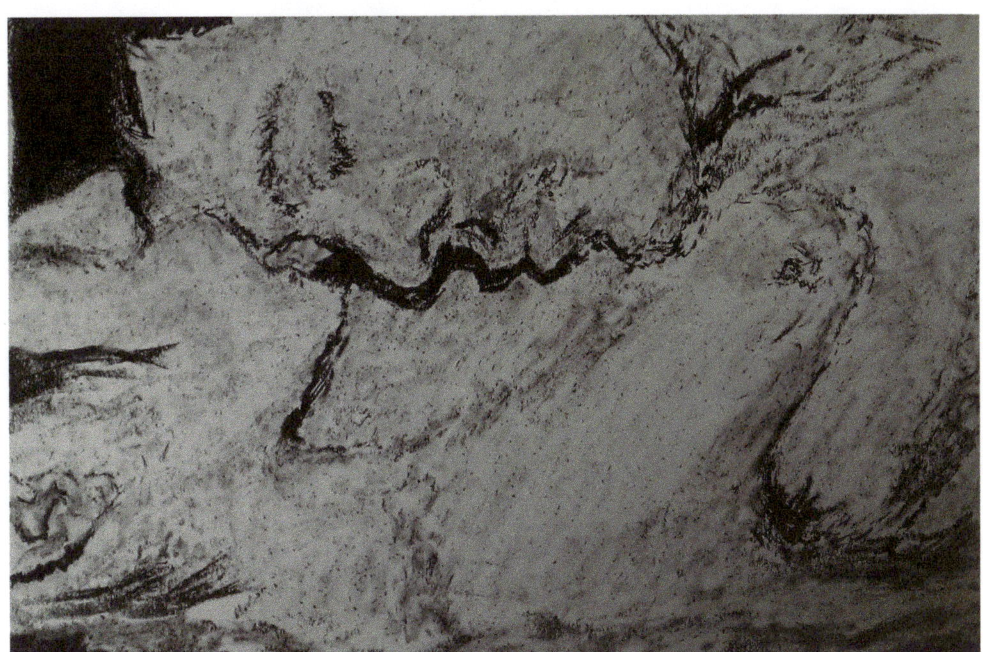

Phoebus
Charcoal on paper.
48.5 x 33 cm. 2012.

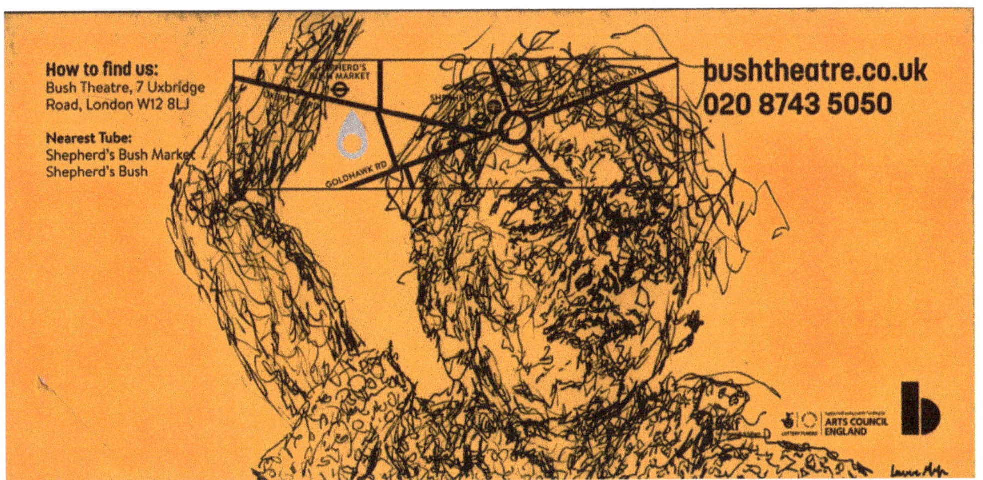

Bush Theatre
A small envelope sized piece of card containing contact details and a little map came with
theatre tickets. Anonymously I drew on it and returned it to the theatre. 2019.

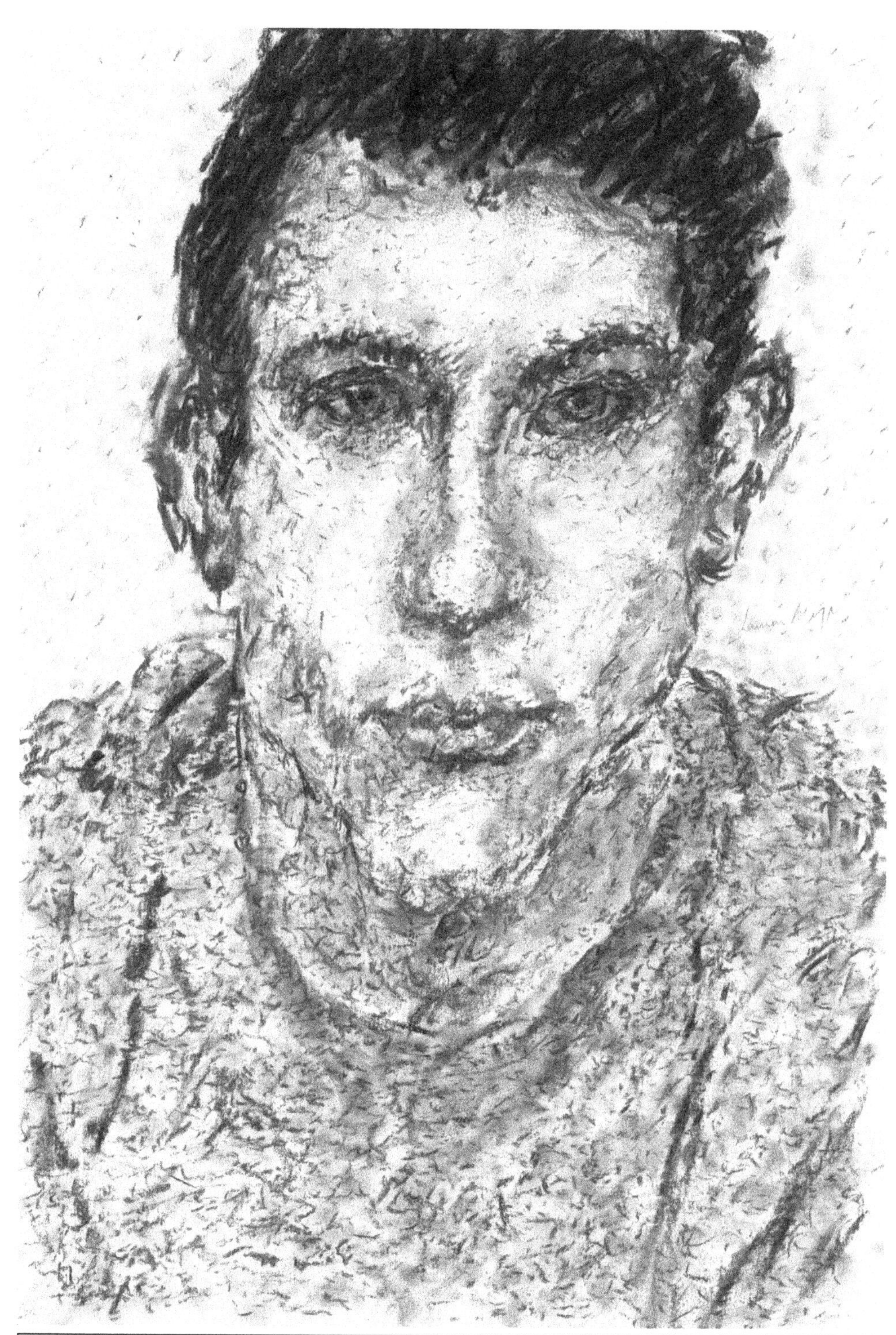

Rhythmics
Charcoal on paper.
21.5 x 33cm. 2012.

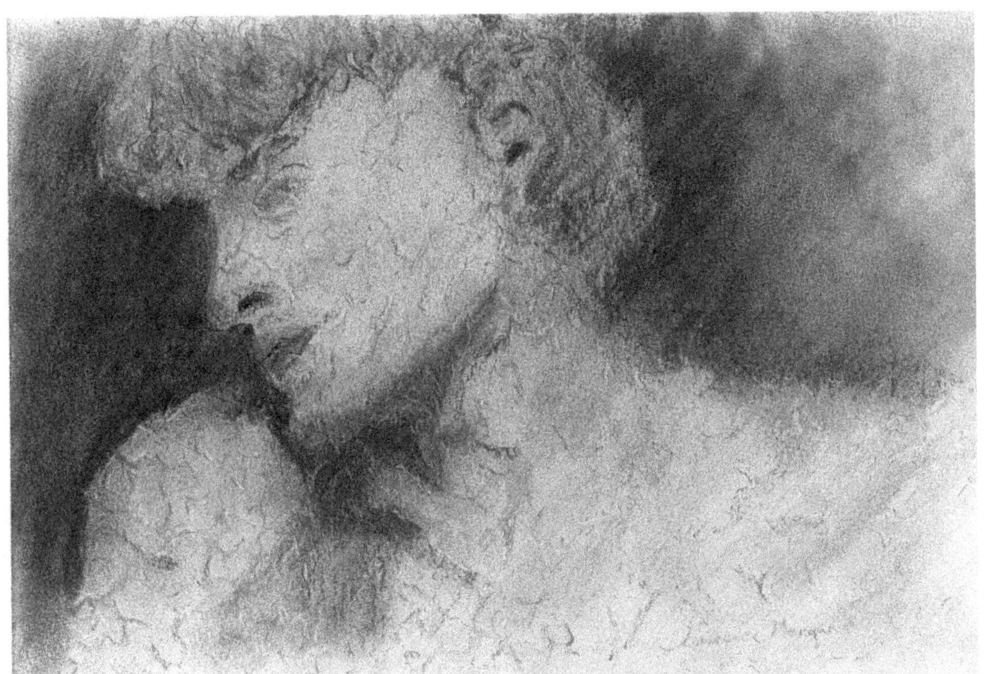

Schrabbelen
Charcoal on paper.
26 x 39 cm. 2012.

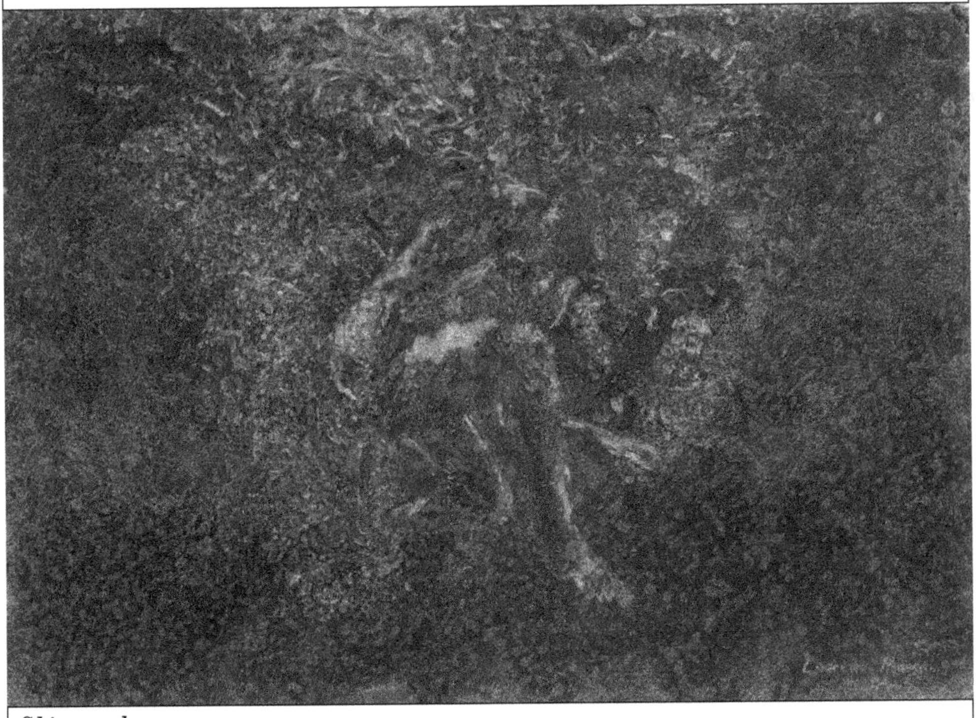

Skimmed
Charcoal on paper.
36 x 25 cm. 2012.

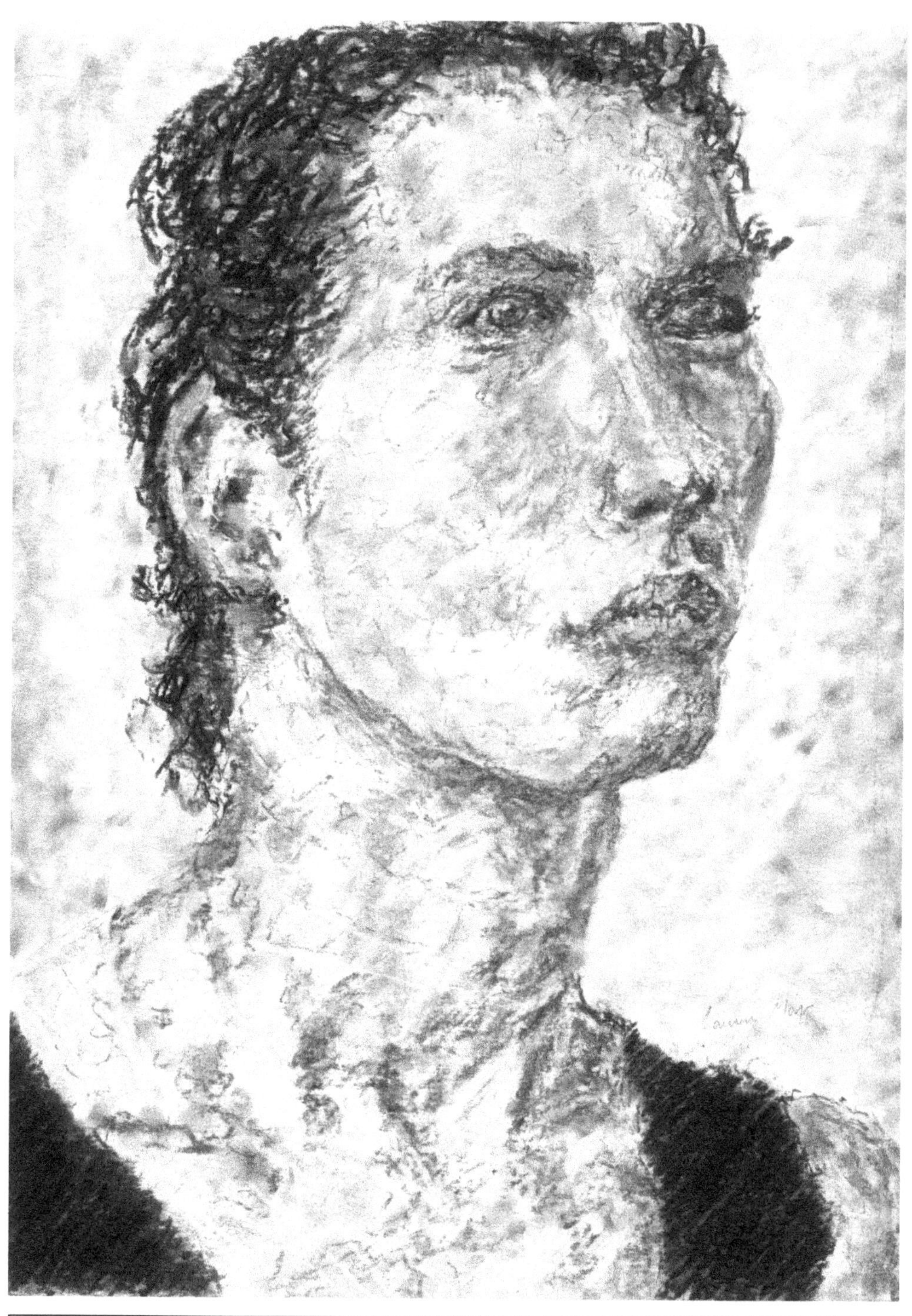

Stemmed
Charcoal on Paper.
21.5 x 29.5 cm.
Year 2012.

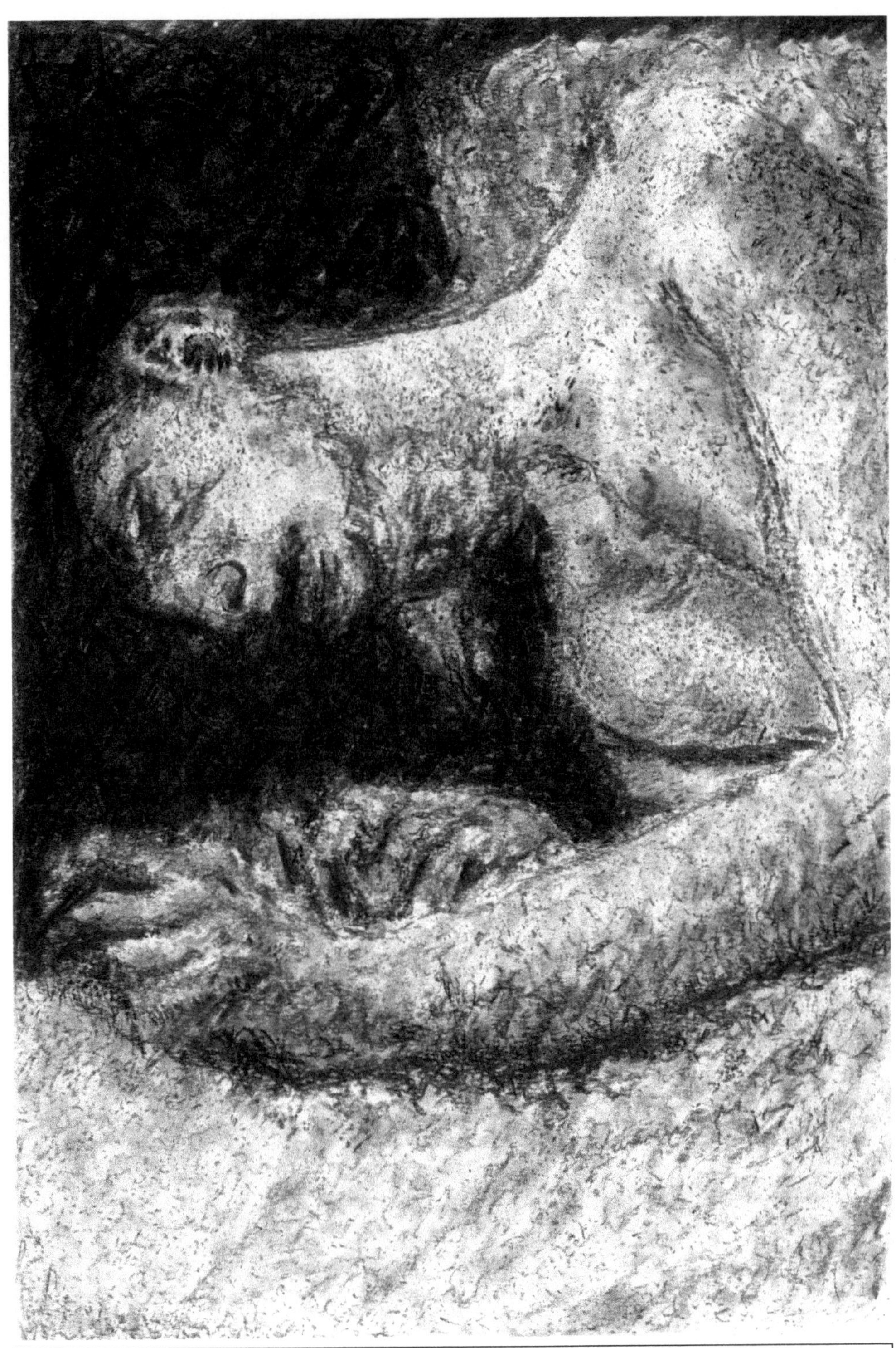

Adrift
Charcoal on paper.
20.5 x 30.5 cm. 2012.

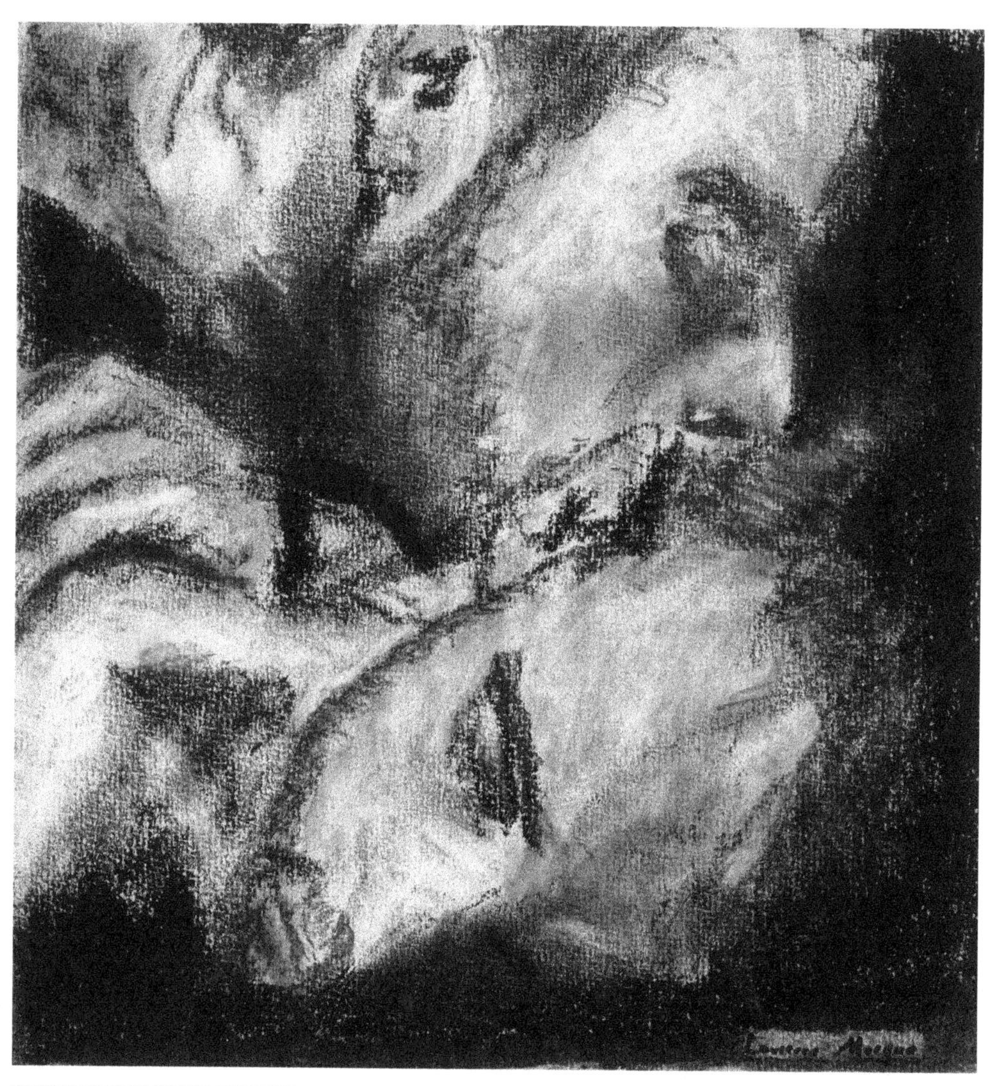

Sweeper
Charcoal on paper.
17.2 x 17.2 cm. 2012.

On page 19 opposite

Undrowned
Charcoal on a manila envelope.
21 x 29.7 cm. 2013.

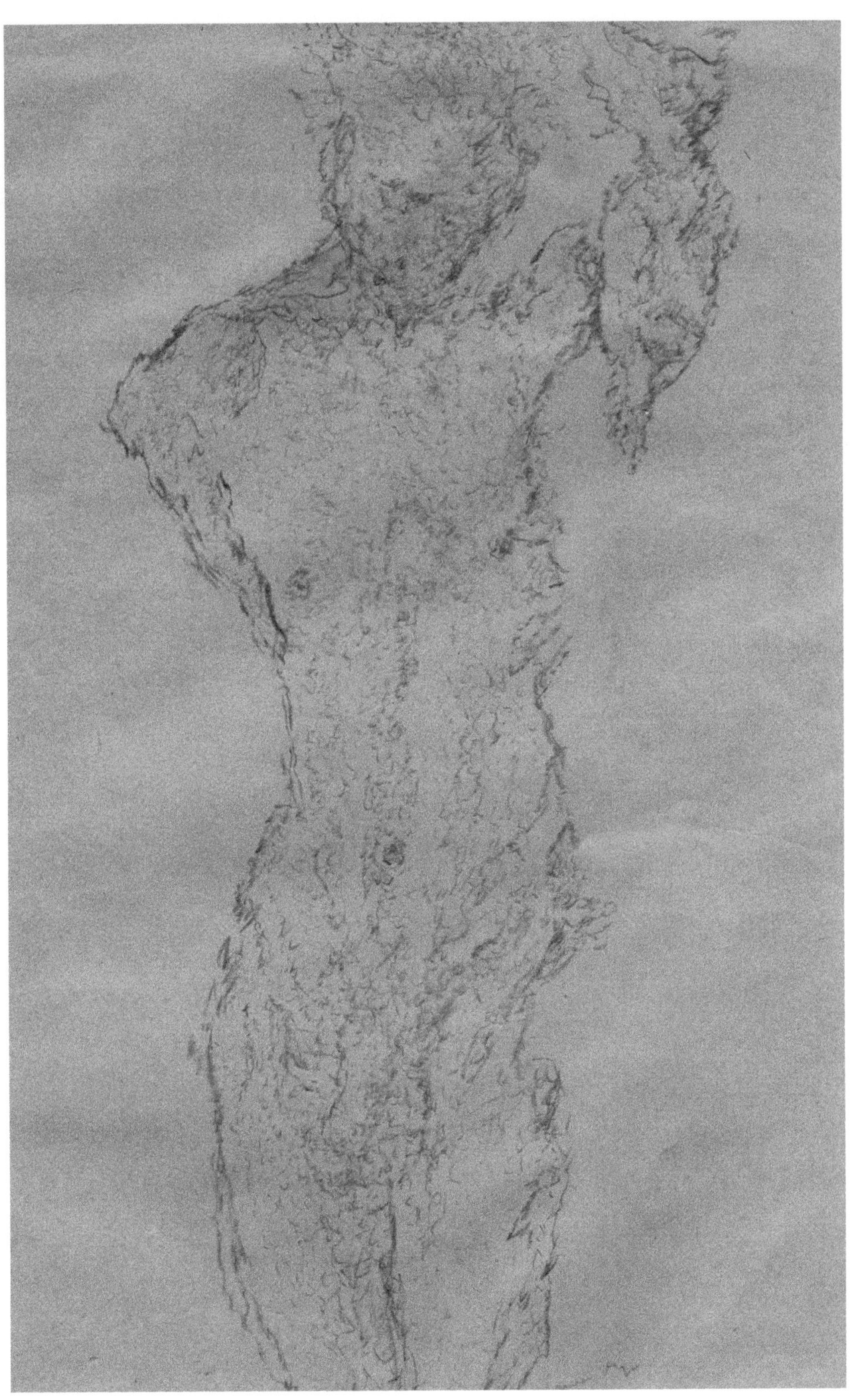

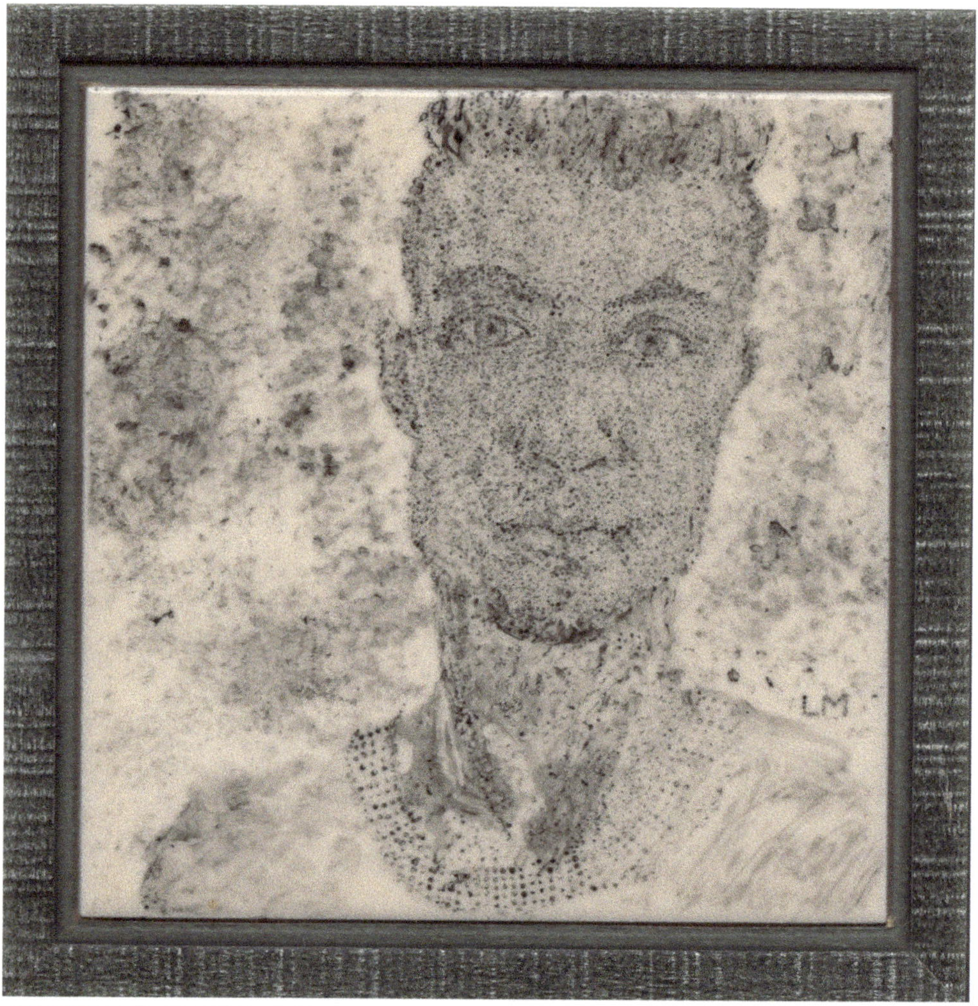

Above:
Tomasz

Below right:
Jimenez

The images on these three pages were created in 2017 using ink on recycled tiles. Each tile is 14.6 x 14.6 cm and they are all framed, The framed size is 17.7 cm square.

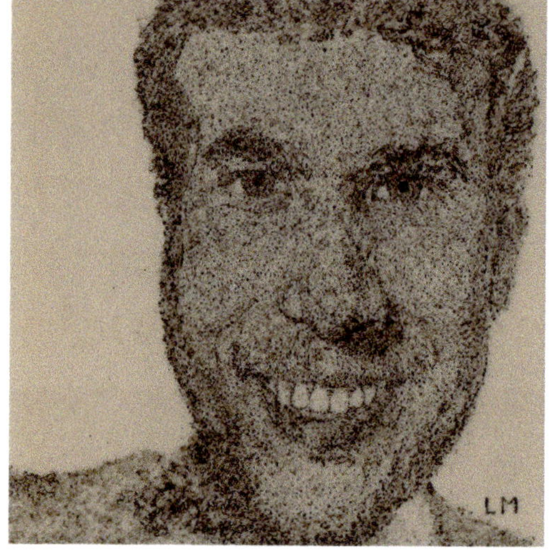

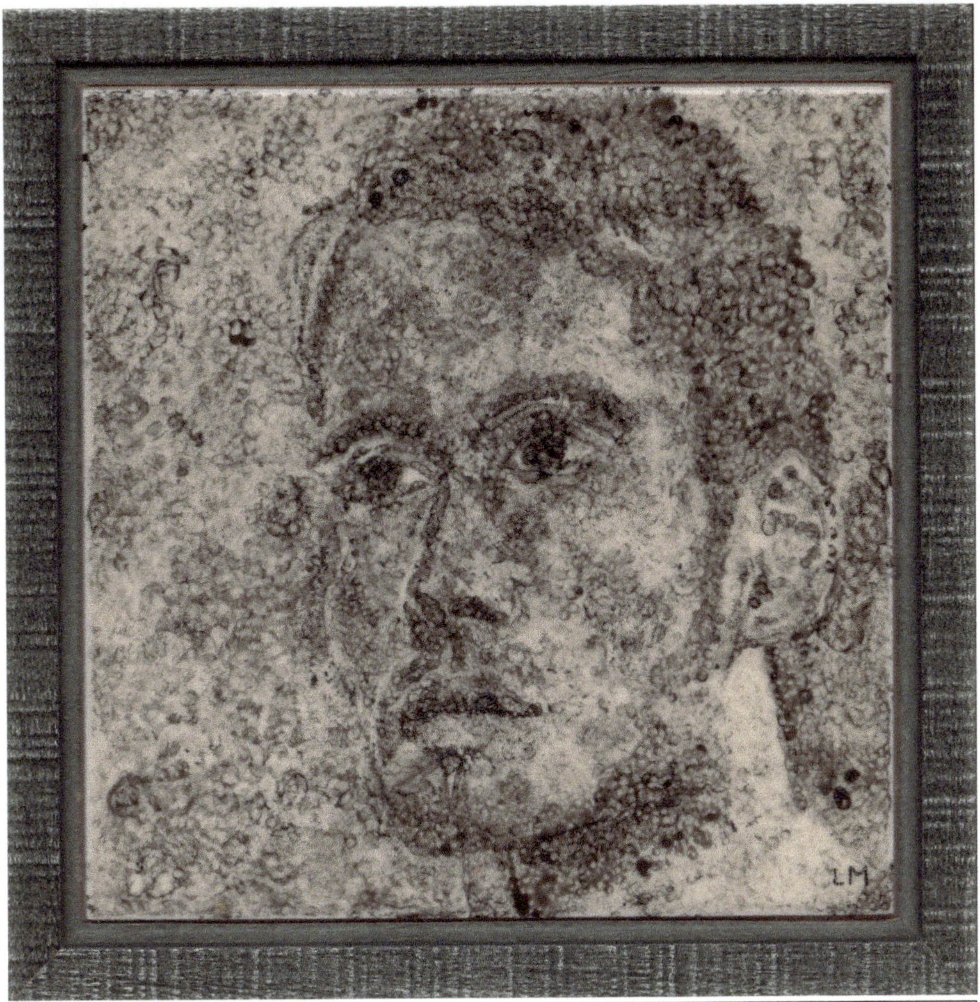

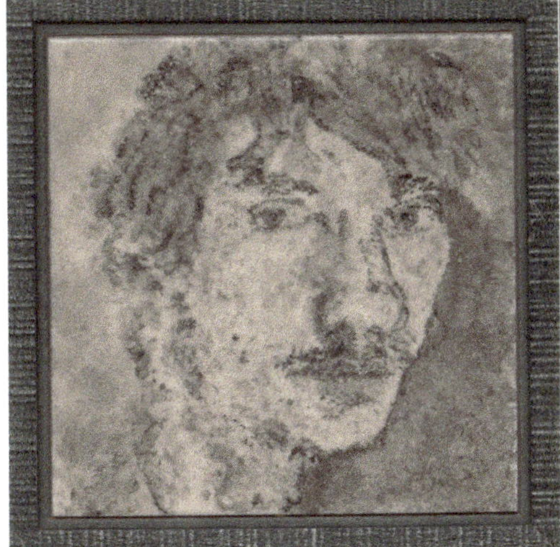

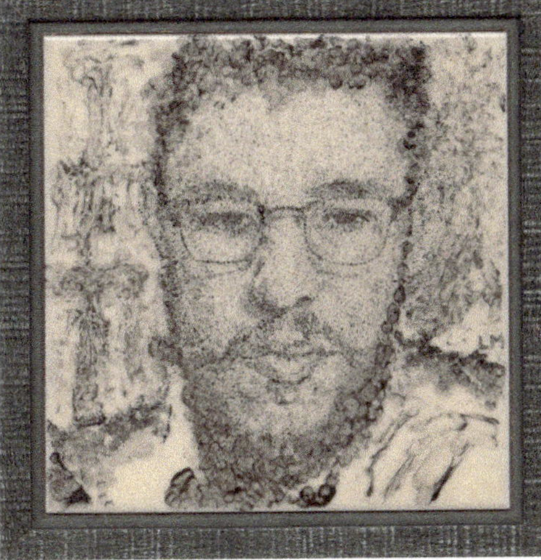

Above: *Alain*
Below left: Giovani
Below right: *Timur the Barman*

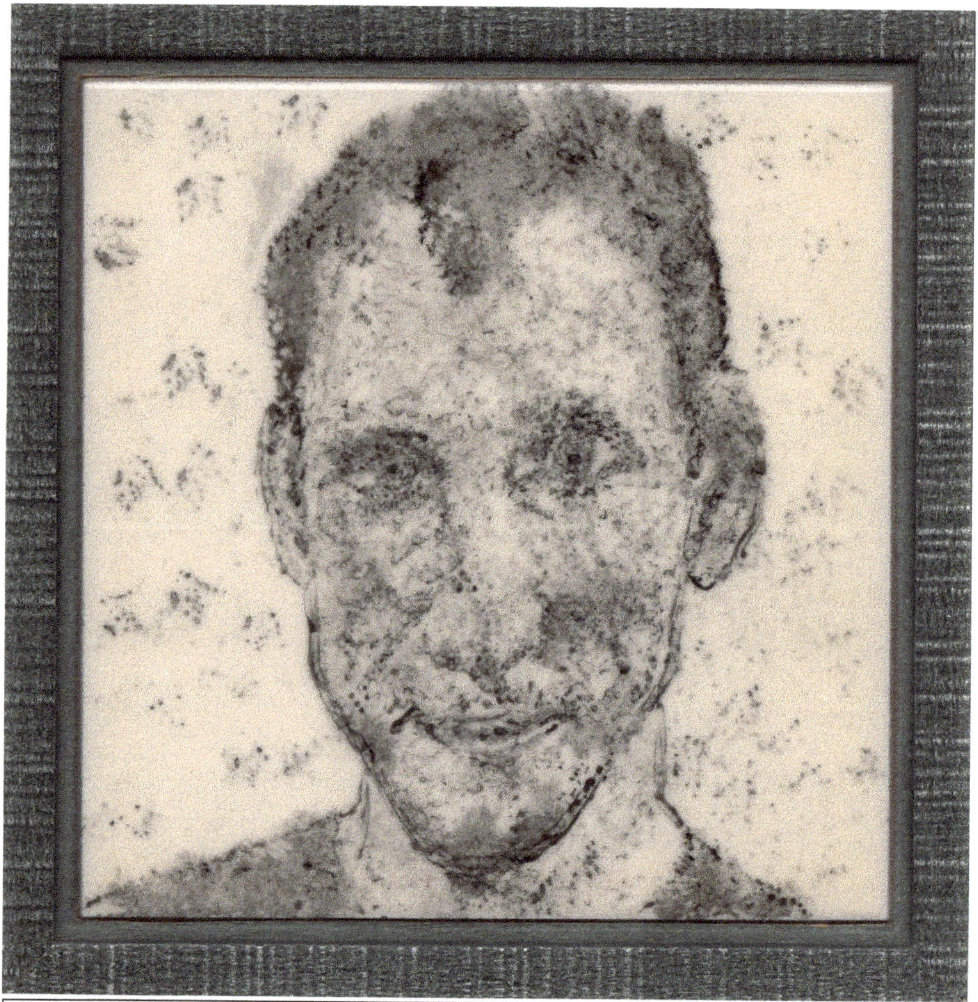

Above: *Andrew*

Below left: *Fabien*   Below right: *Ridges*

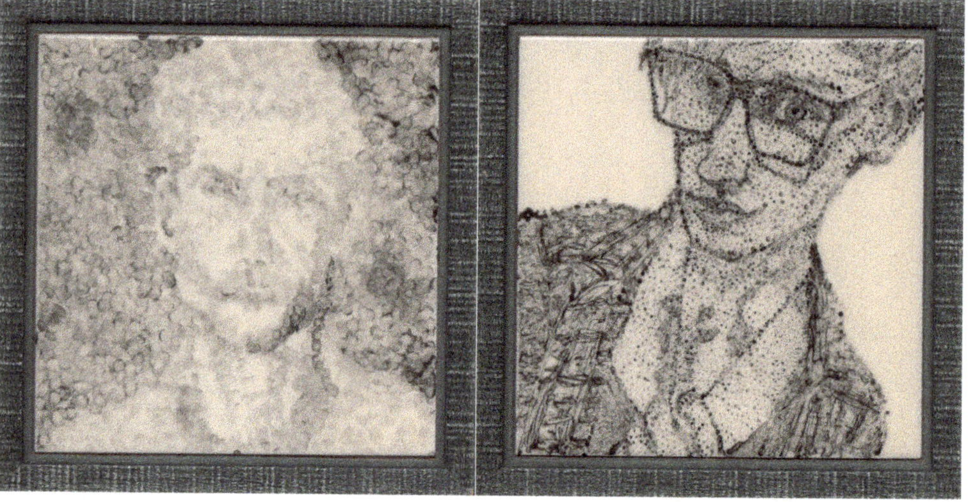

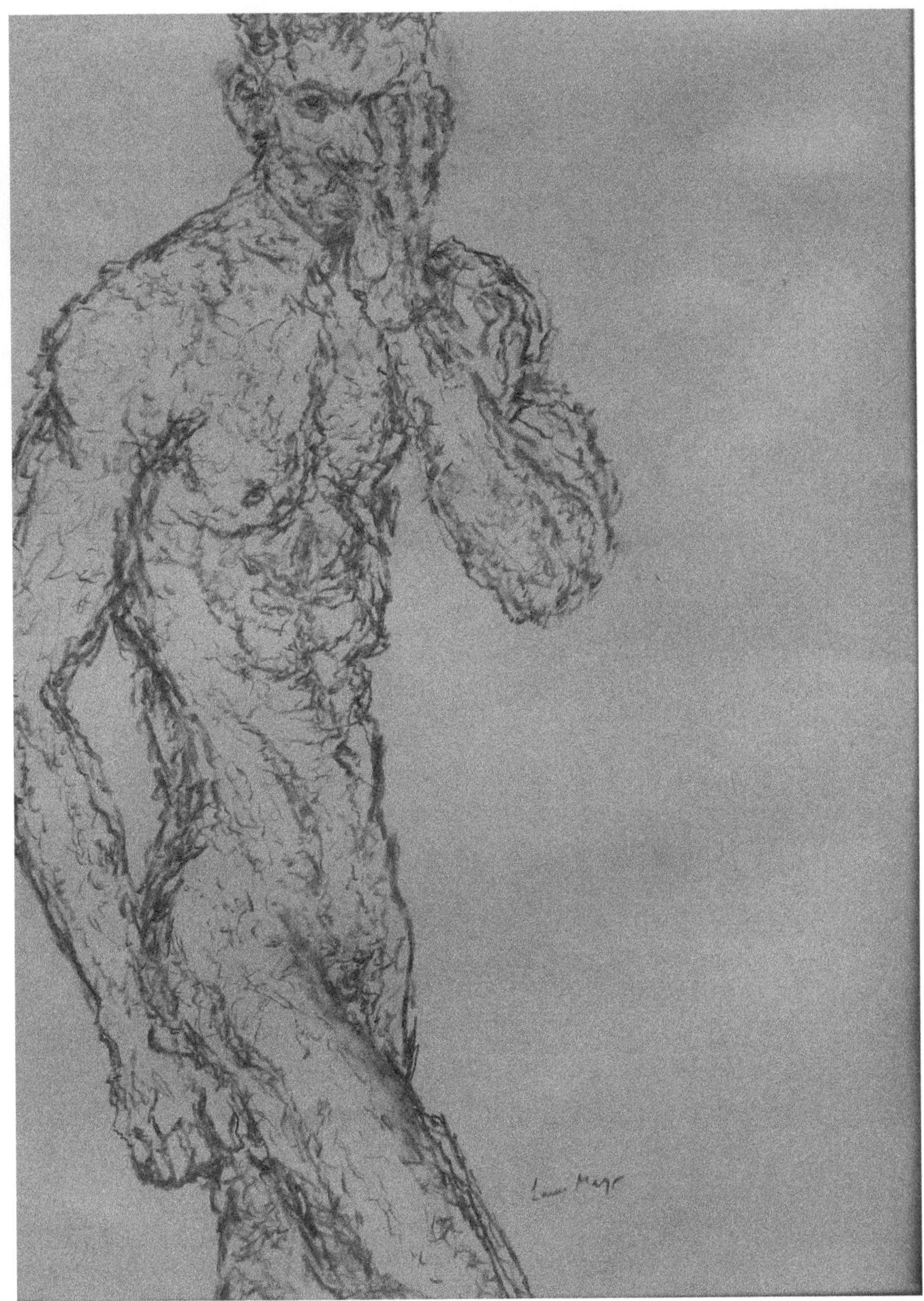

Dauntless
Charcoal on a manila envelope.
21 x 29.7 cm. 2013.

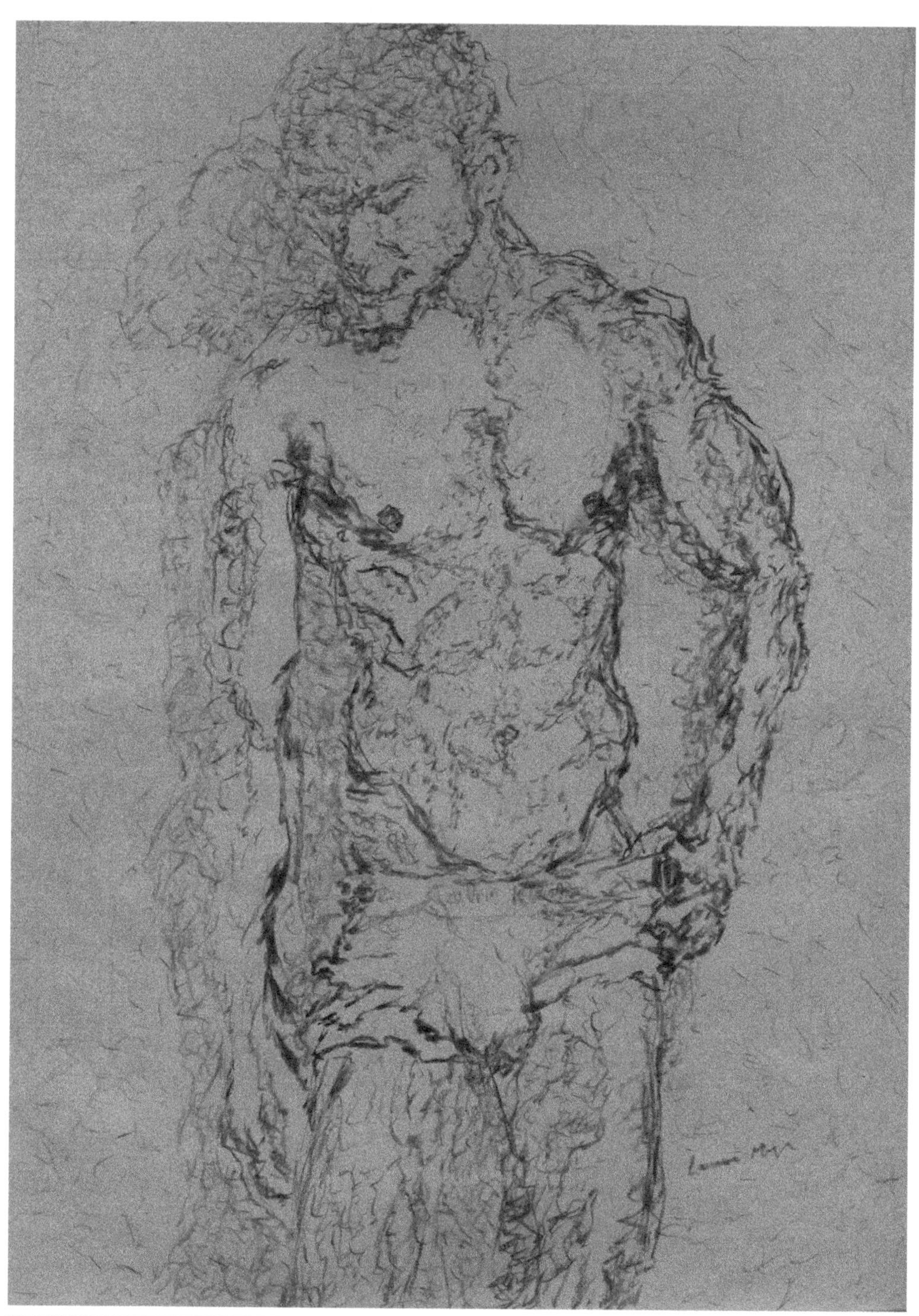

FAO
Charcoal on a manila envelope. 21 x 29.7 cm. 2013.

Opposite: *Deliverance*
Charcoal on cardboard, with a spray paint white wash and a distressed card background. 60 x 92 cm. 2013.

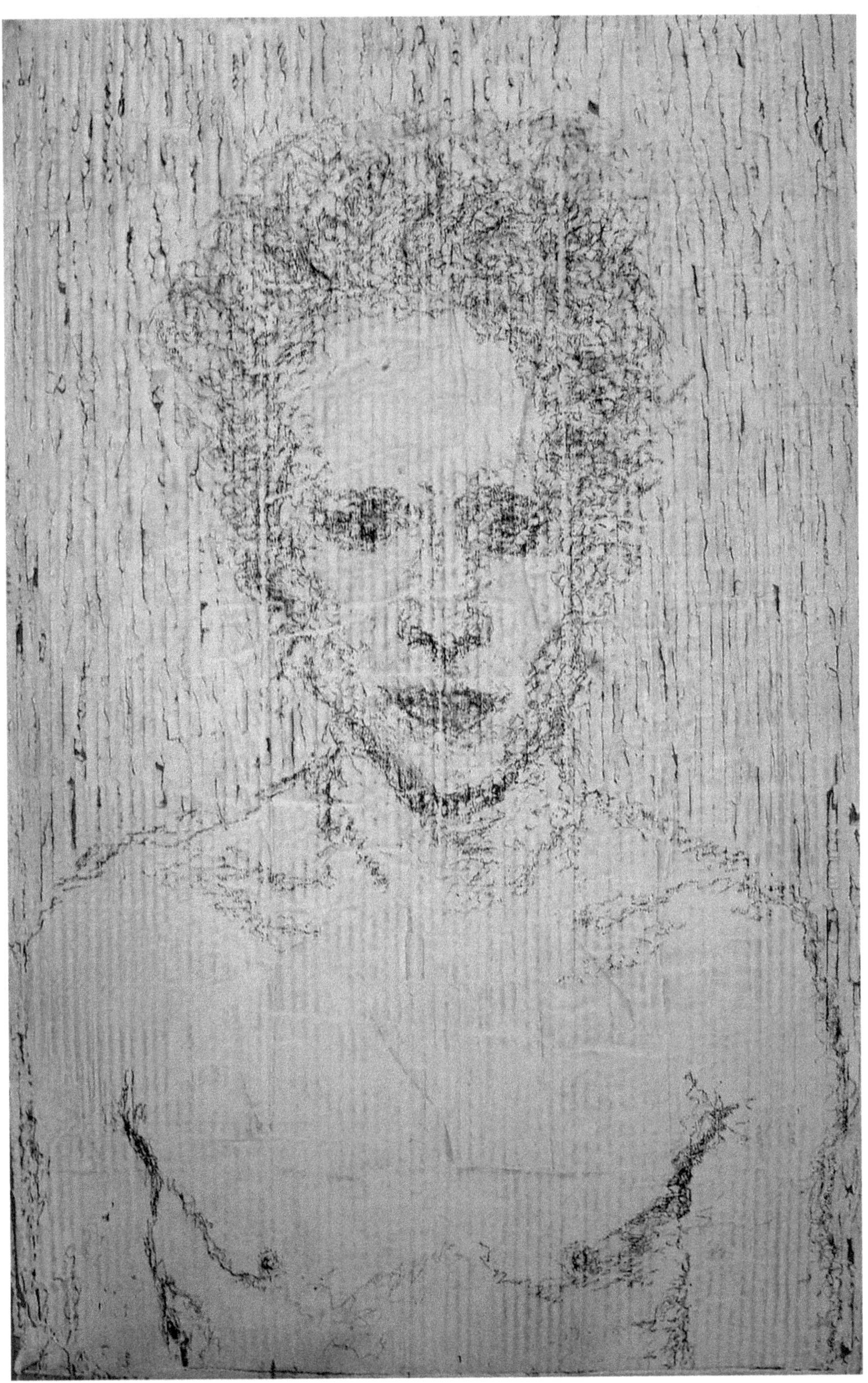

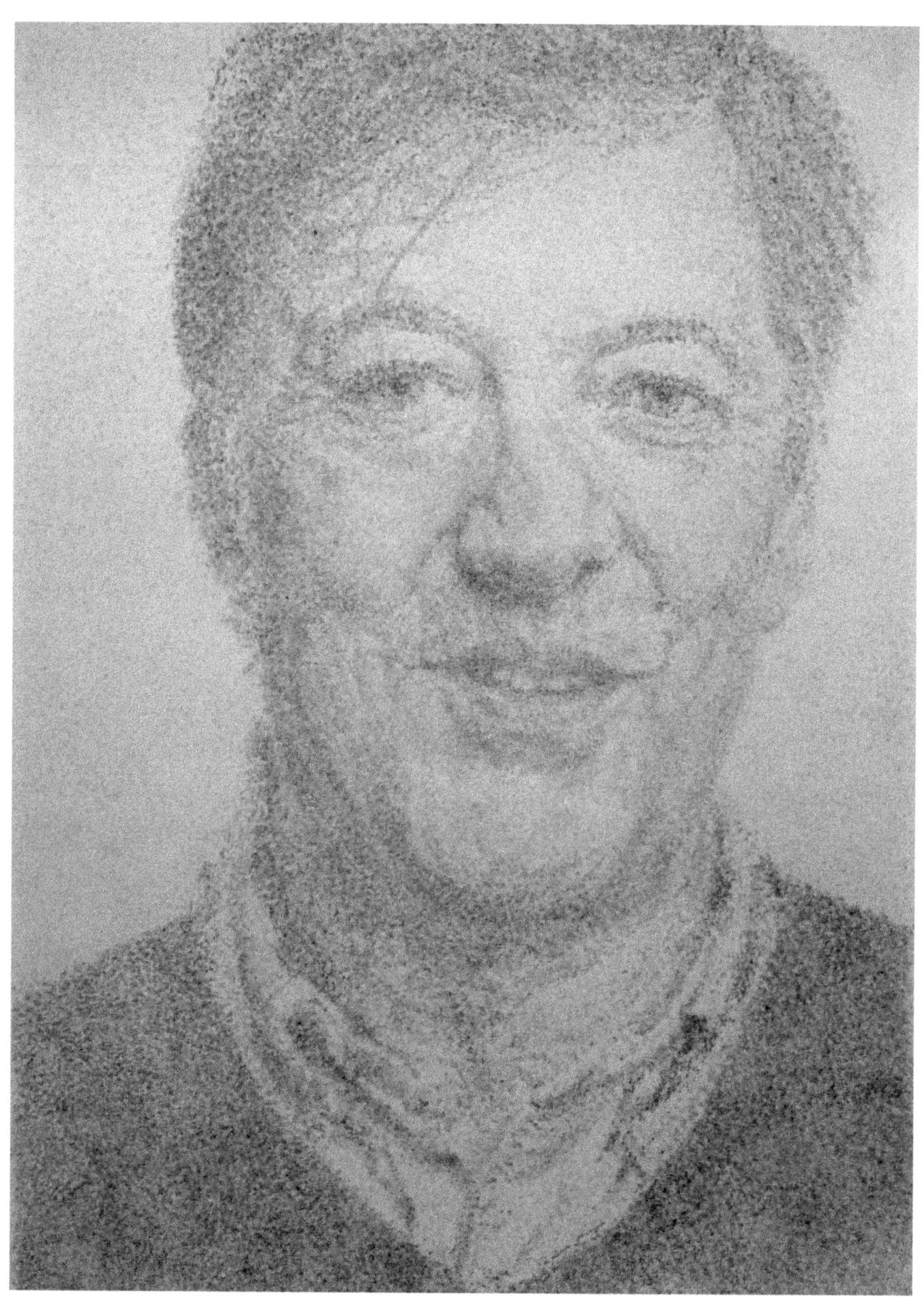

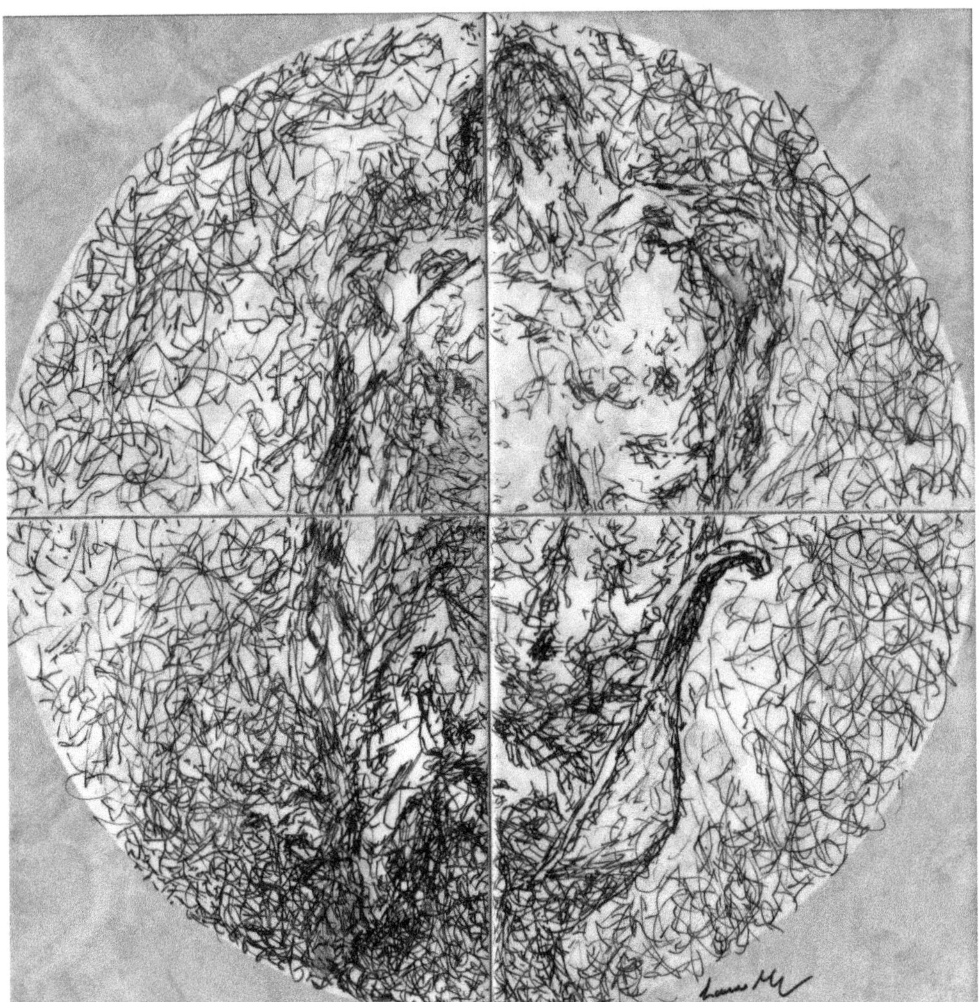

Latter Days
Ink over four recycled tiles.
29.7 x 29.7 cm

Opposite on page 26.
Fry
Charcoal on paper 39.2 x 55.3 cm (53.4 x 70.3 inc. frame). 2013.
A larger piece I started, not knowing what it would entail or what it would come to mean to me. I worked through the night for 10 weeks on a small kitchen table taken up by the paper. I was fuelled by energy drinks and at times, what I felt was mania. I had started so I had to continue what was a real exploration for me.
I later learned the technique was pointillism and I was constantly adding elements of depth, never knowing when to stop. Nervousness often had me fearful to sign pieces, as if I would be mocked for daring to attribute pride in creation. My small signature appears where his jumper overlaps shirt.

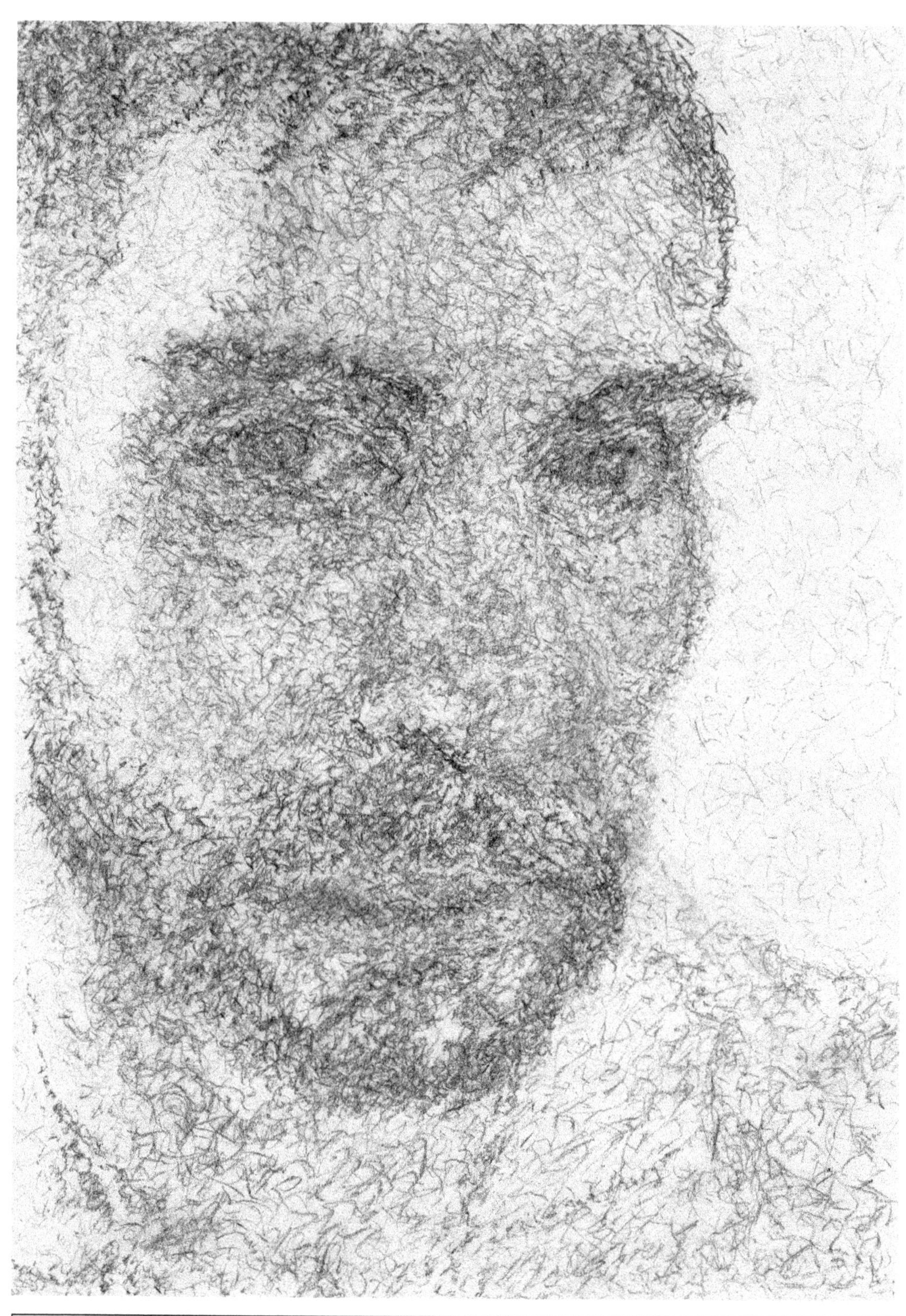

Kelp
Graphite on a postcard.
20.5 x 29.3 cm. 2013.

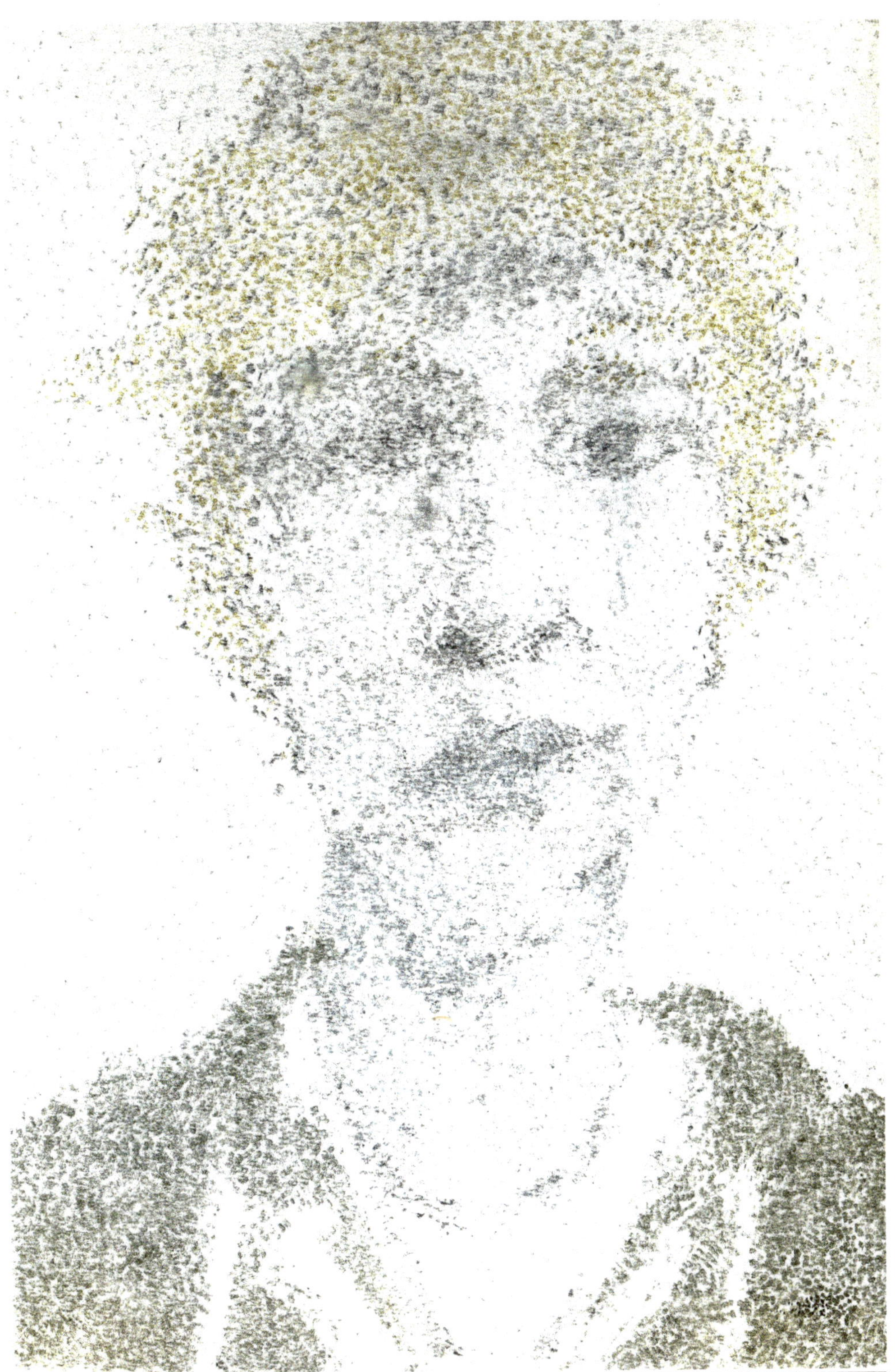

Nikko
Coloured charcoal pencils on paper. 2013.

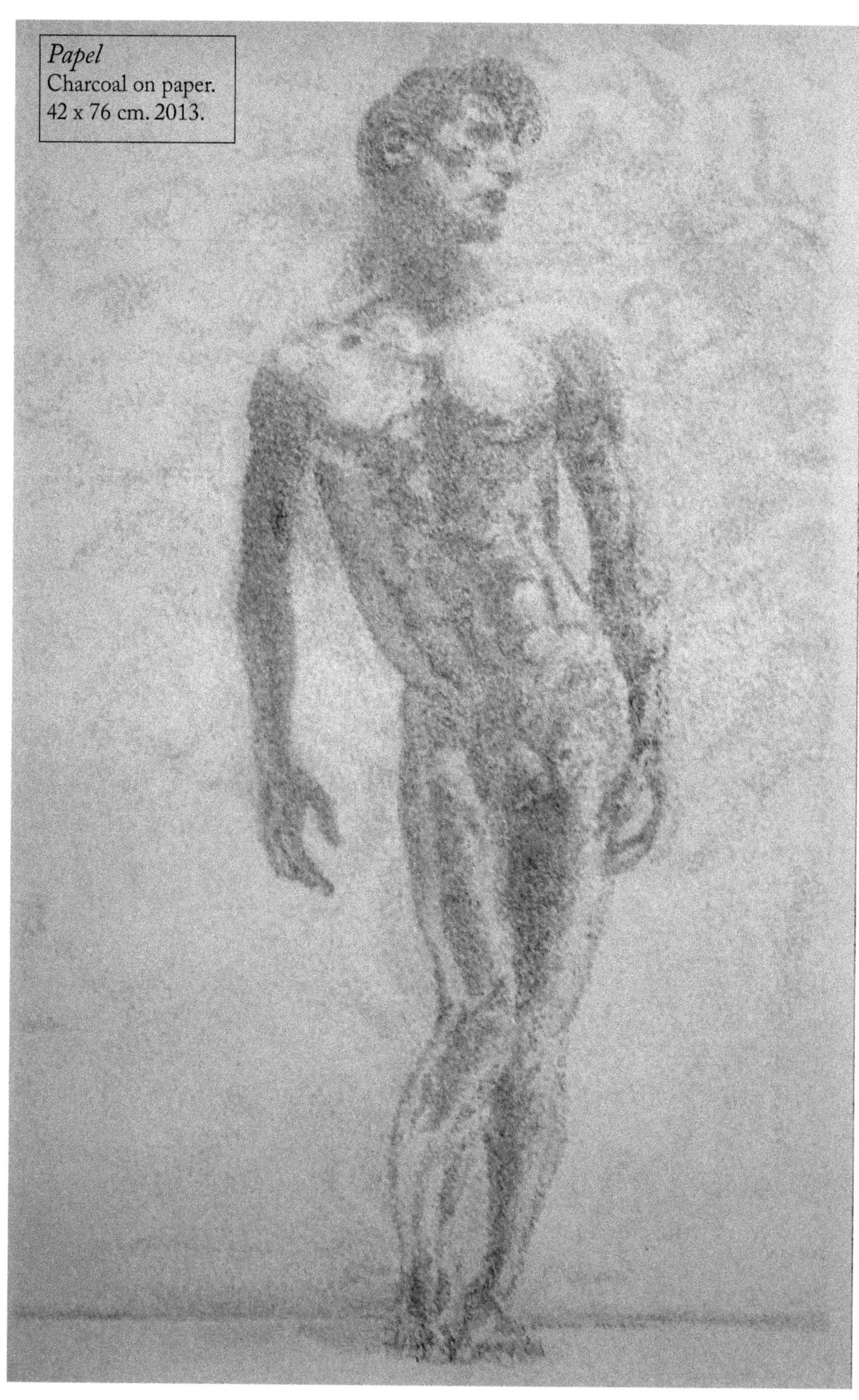

Papel
Charcoal on paper.
42 x 76 cm. 2013.

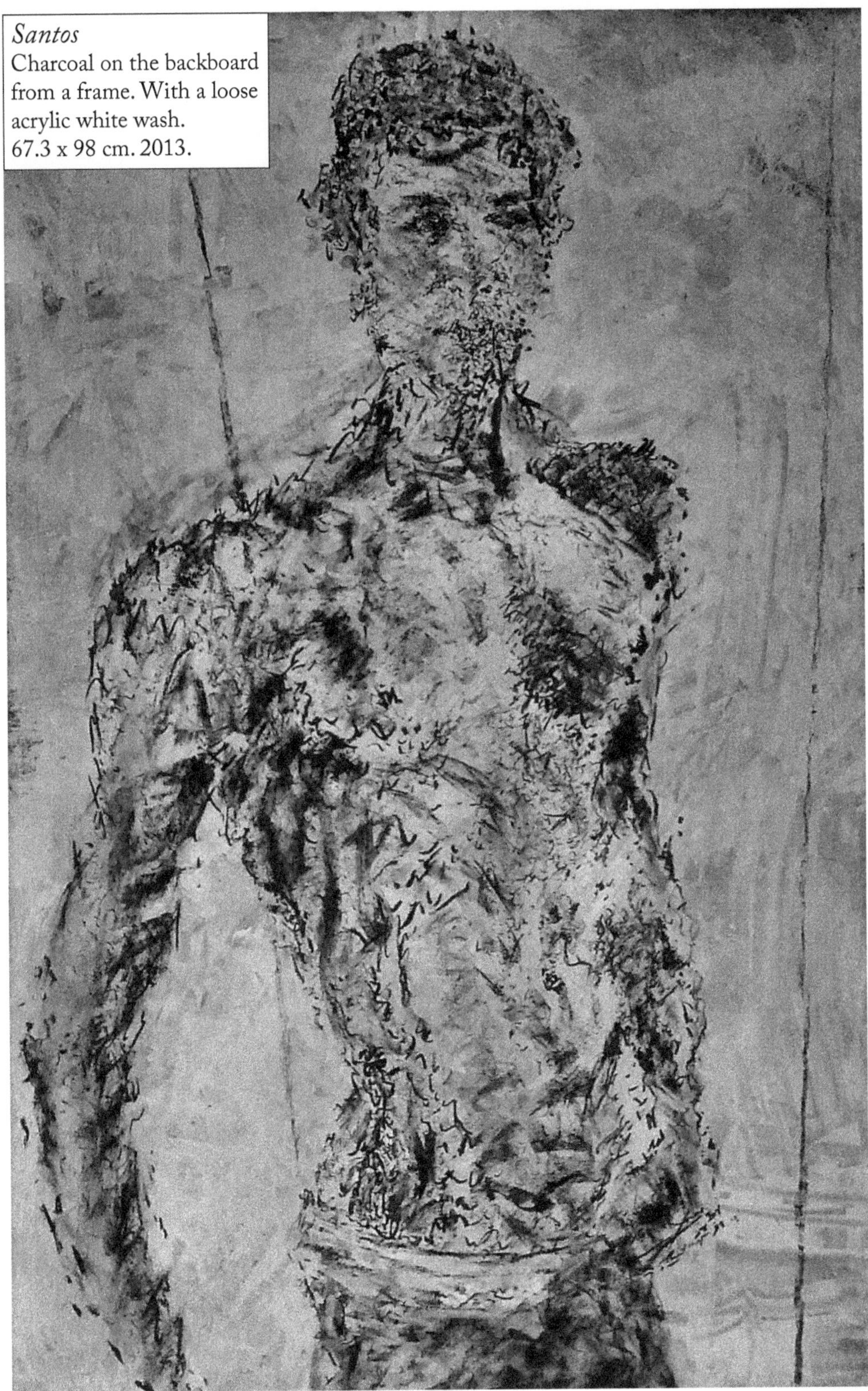

Santos
Charcoal on the backboard from a frame. With a loose acrylic white wash.
67.3 x 98 cm. 2013.

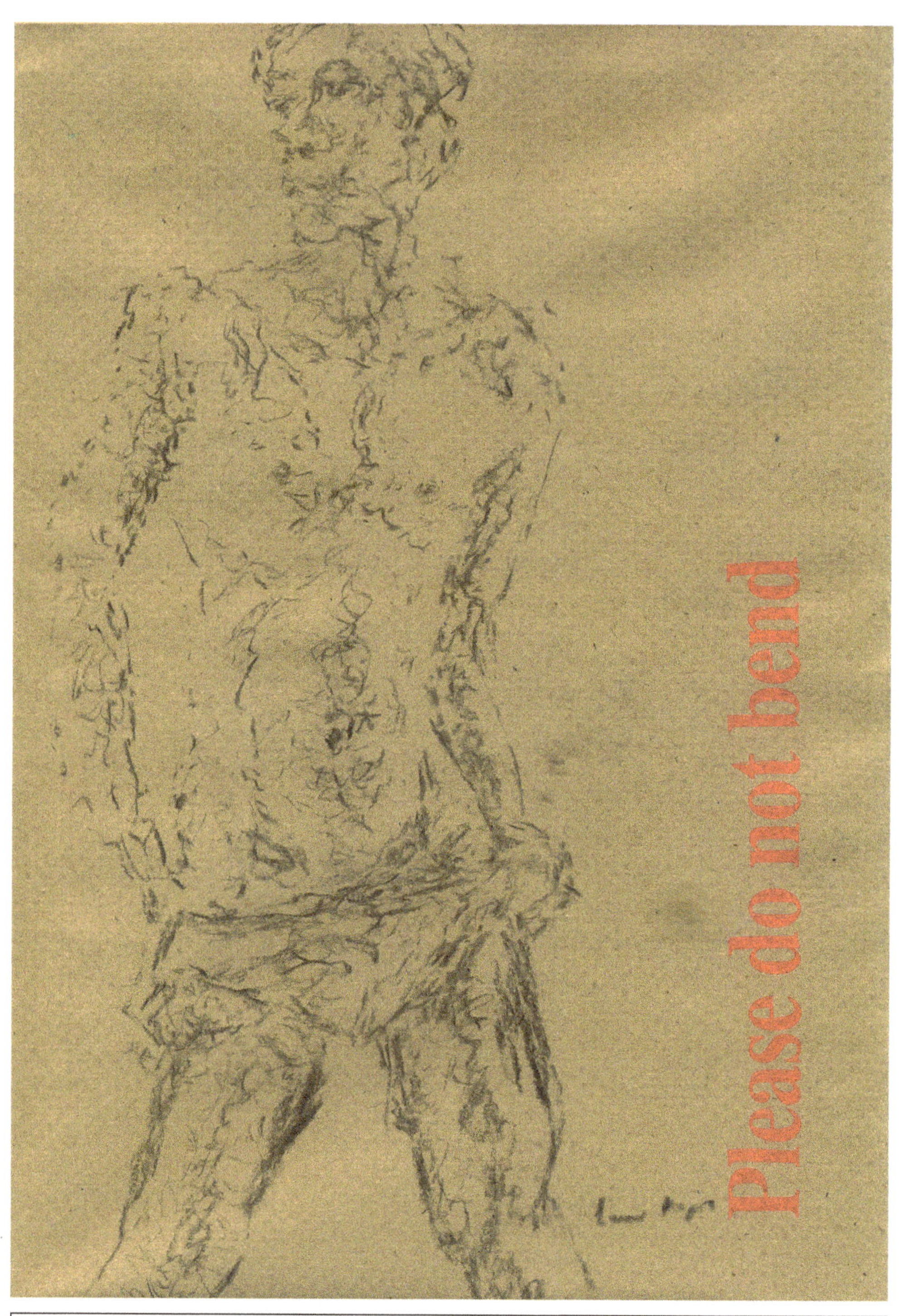

With A Little Feeling
Charcoal on a manila envelope that reads 'Please do not bend' up the right side.
14.8 x 21 cm. 2013.

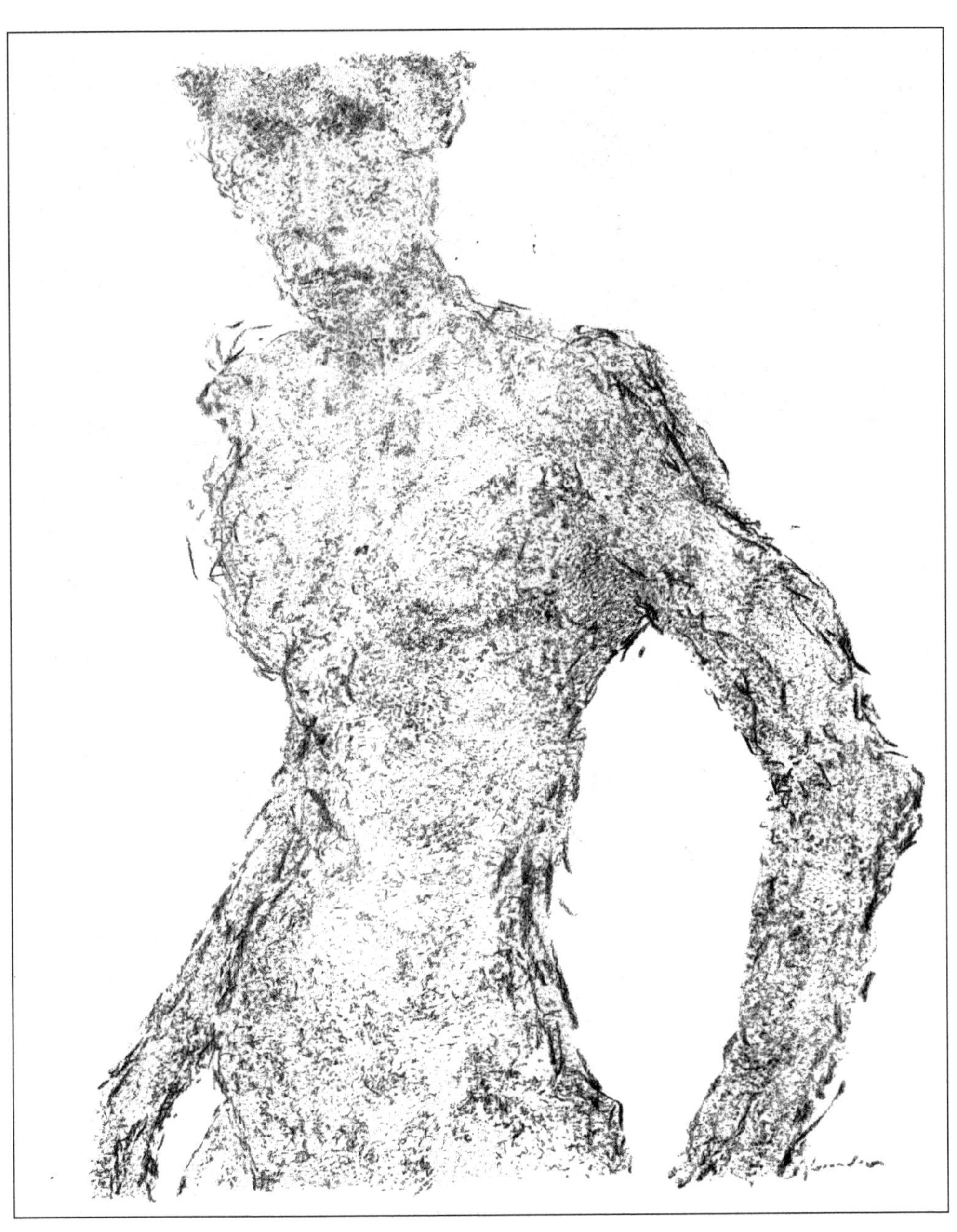

Tangle
Charcoal on paper.
26.5 x 34.2 cm. 2013.

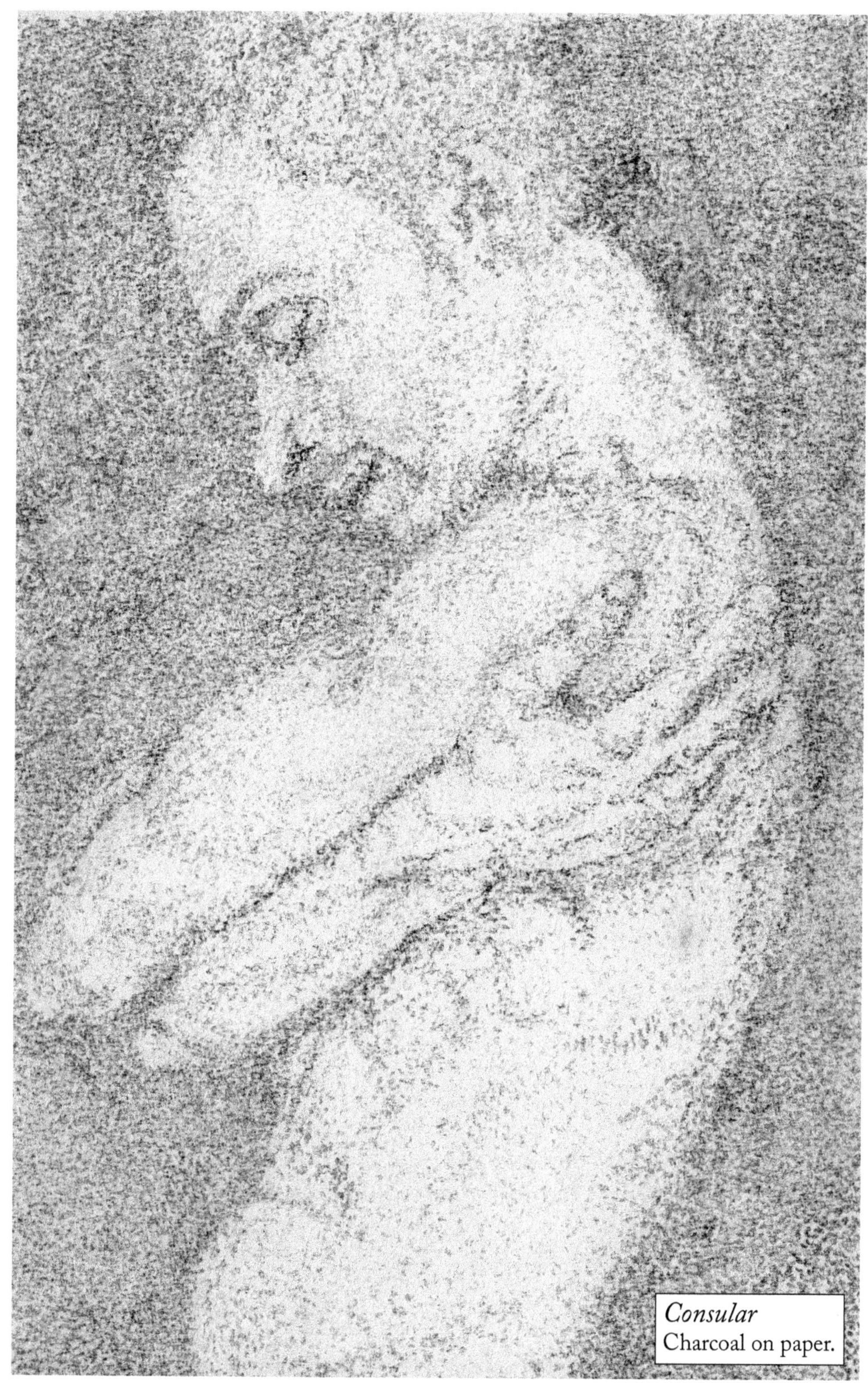

Consular
Charcoal on paper.

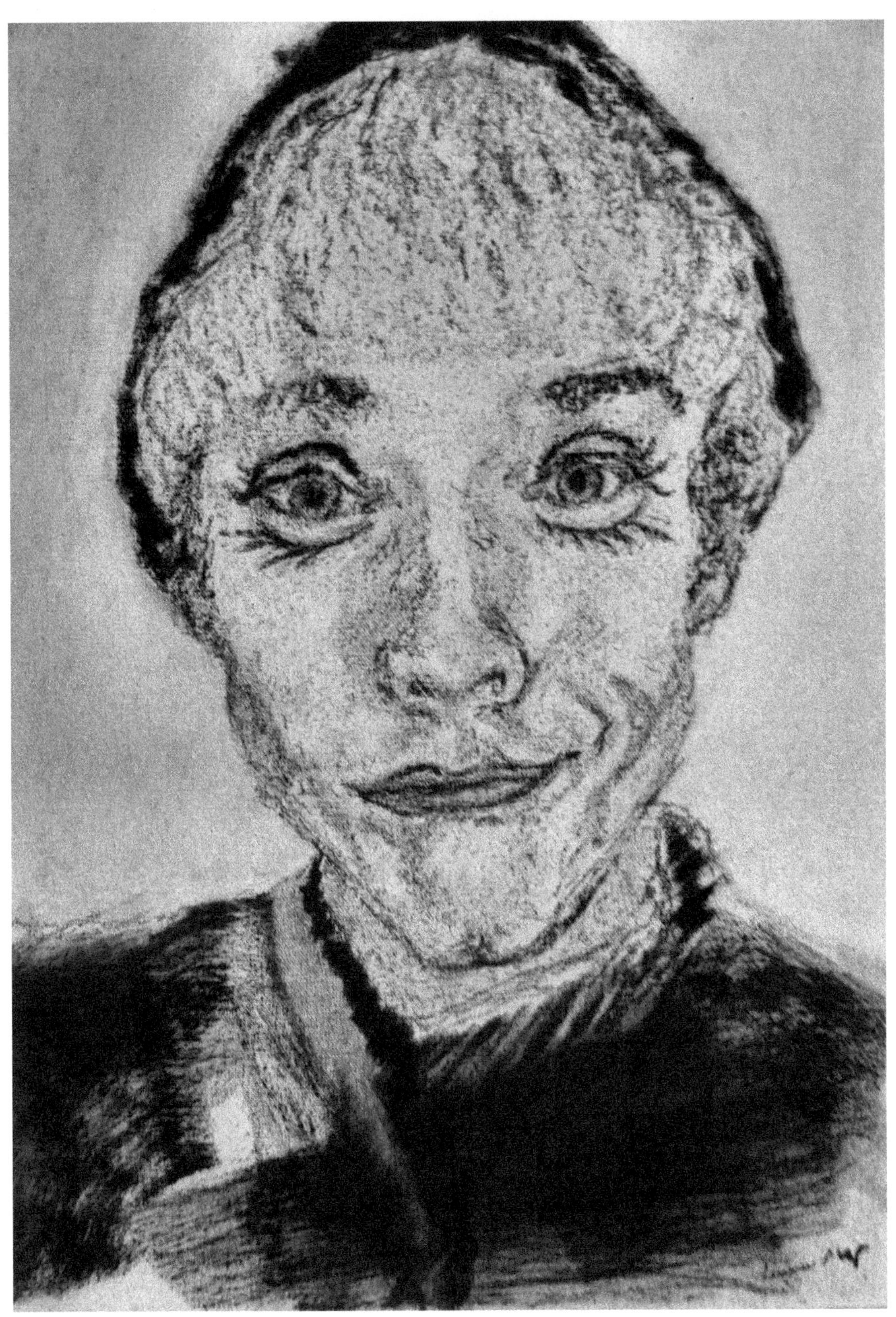

Alfie Ordinary
Charcoal On Canvas. 40.5 x 50.5 cm. 2015.
My first experiment with charcoal on canvas. A drag artist who's work I adore.

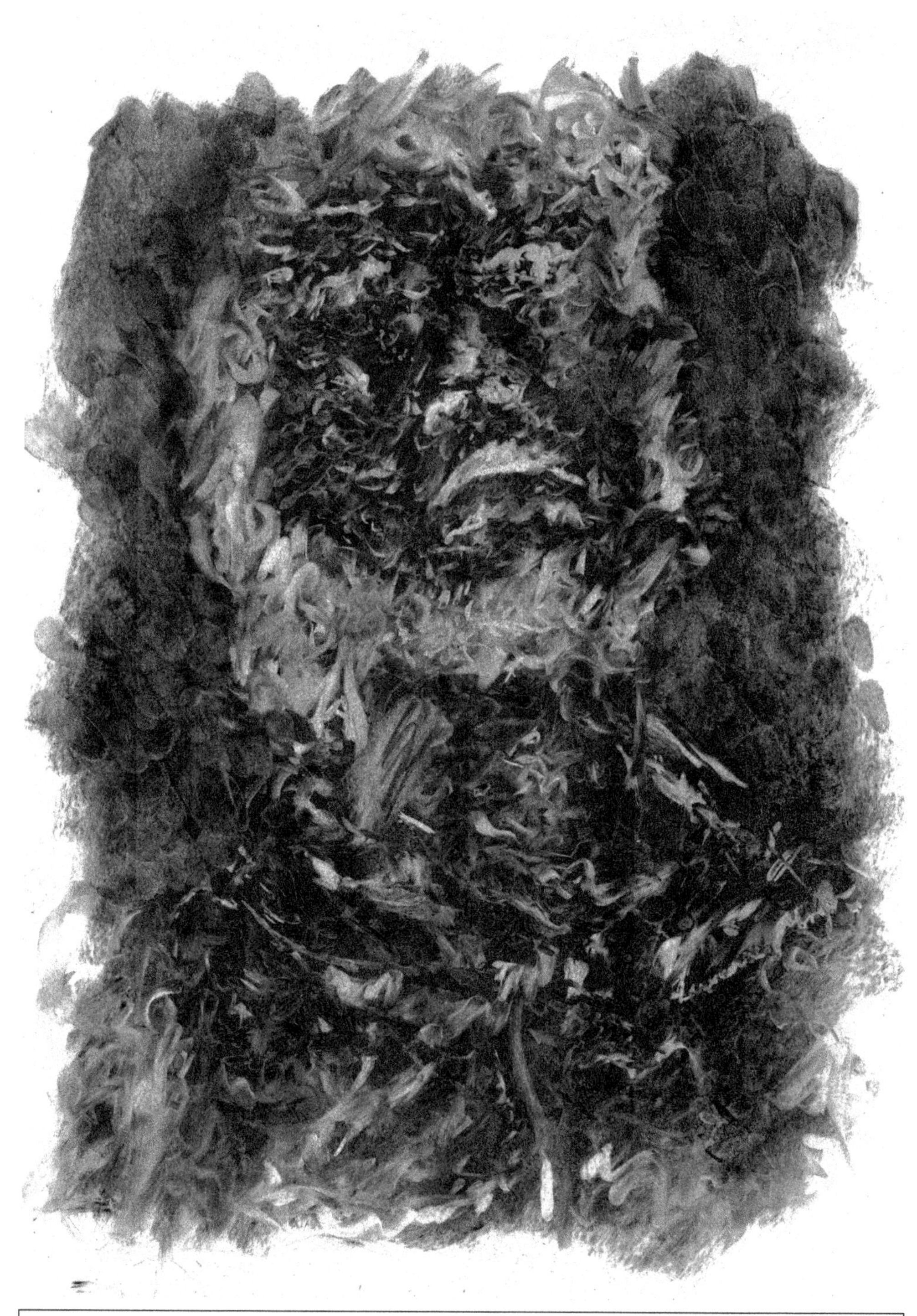

Sapling
Charcoal on paper.
29.5 x 39.5 cm.

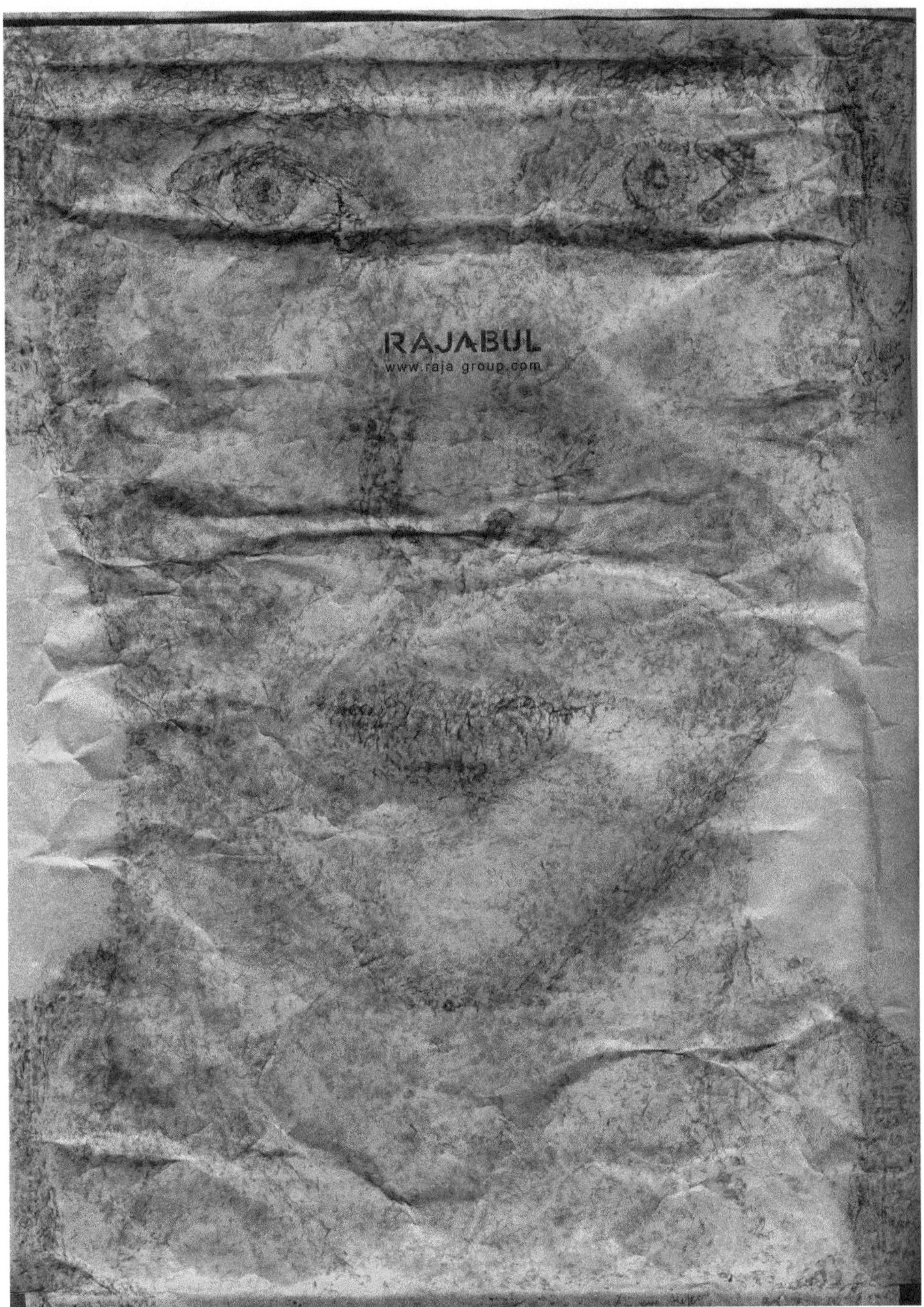

Anvil
Charcoal on a used jiffy bag.
19.4 x 32 cm (17.2 x 39.7 including frame). 2016.
I love this pointillist portrait and how it works with the creases and shadows that are cast on this canvas. I like minimising my ecological impact and am fortunate, I feel, that this adds to my pleasure creating and hopefully affords my work an intrigue.

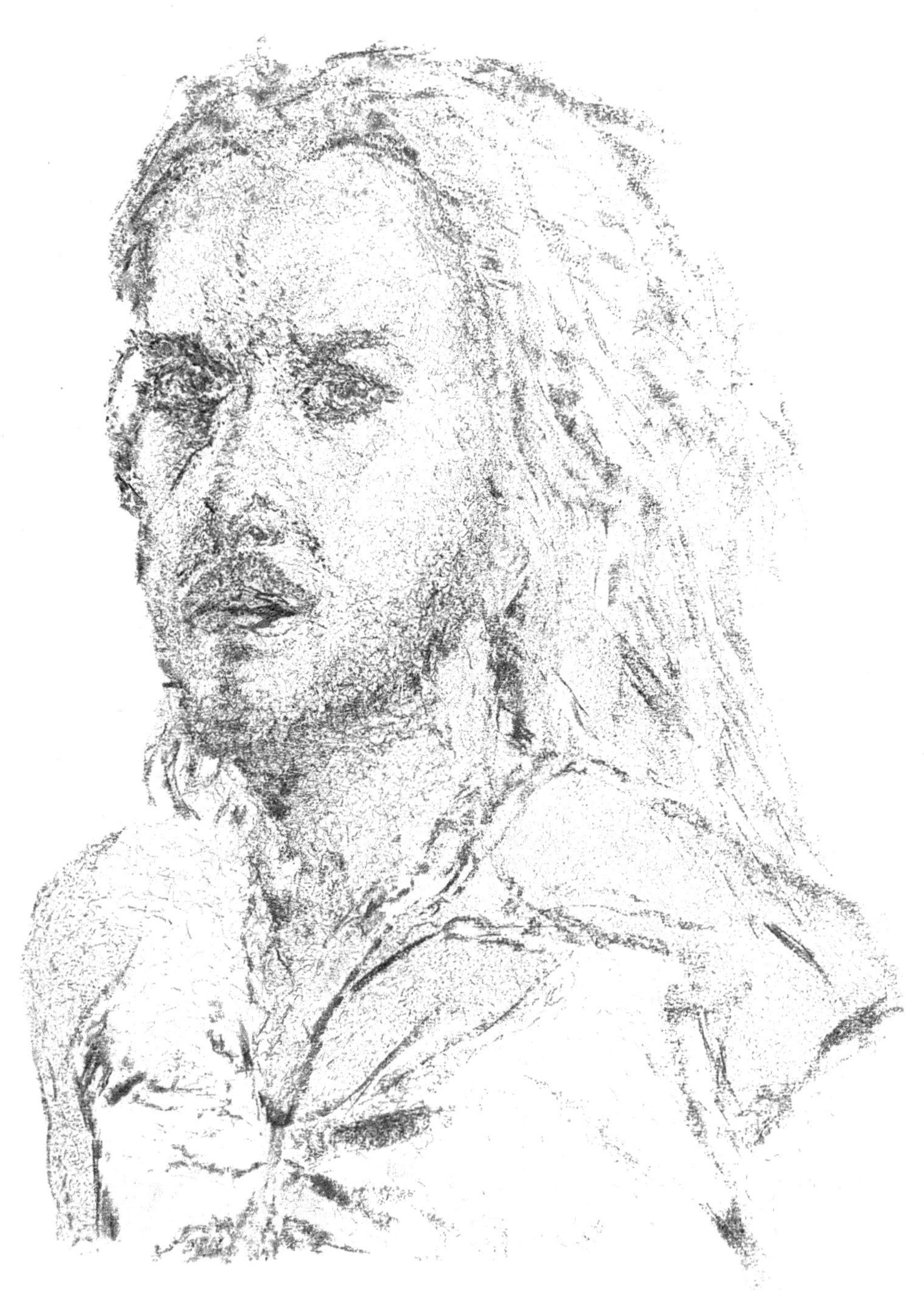

Tim
Charcoal on paper.
29.7 x 42 cm. 2017.
A study of Tim Michin

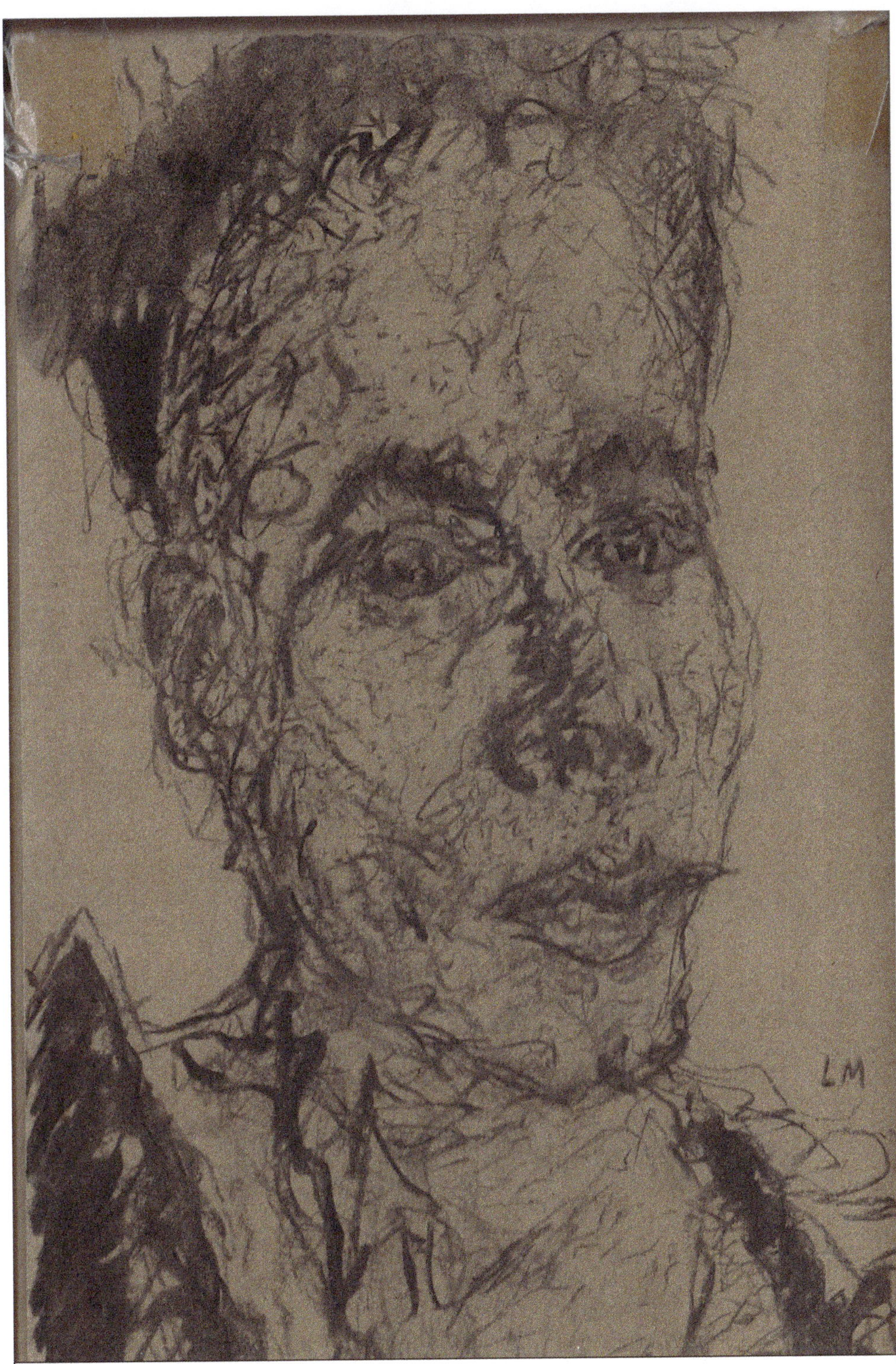

Shelter
Charcoal on a recycled but intact box.
16.5 x 28.2 (...x 16.5) cm. 2018.

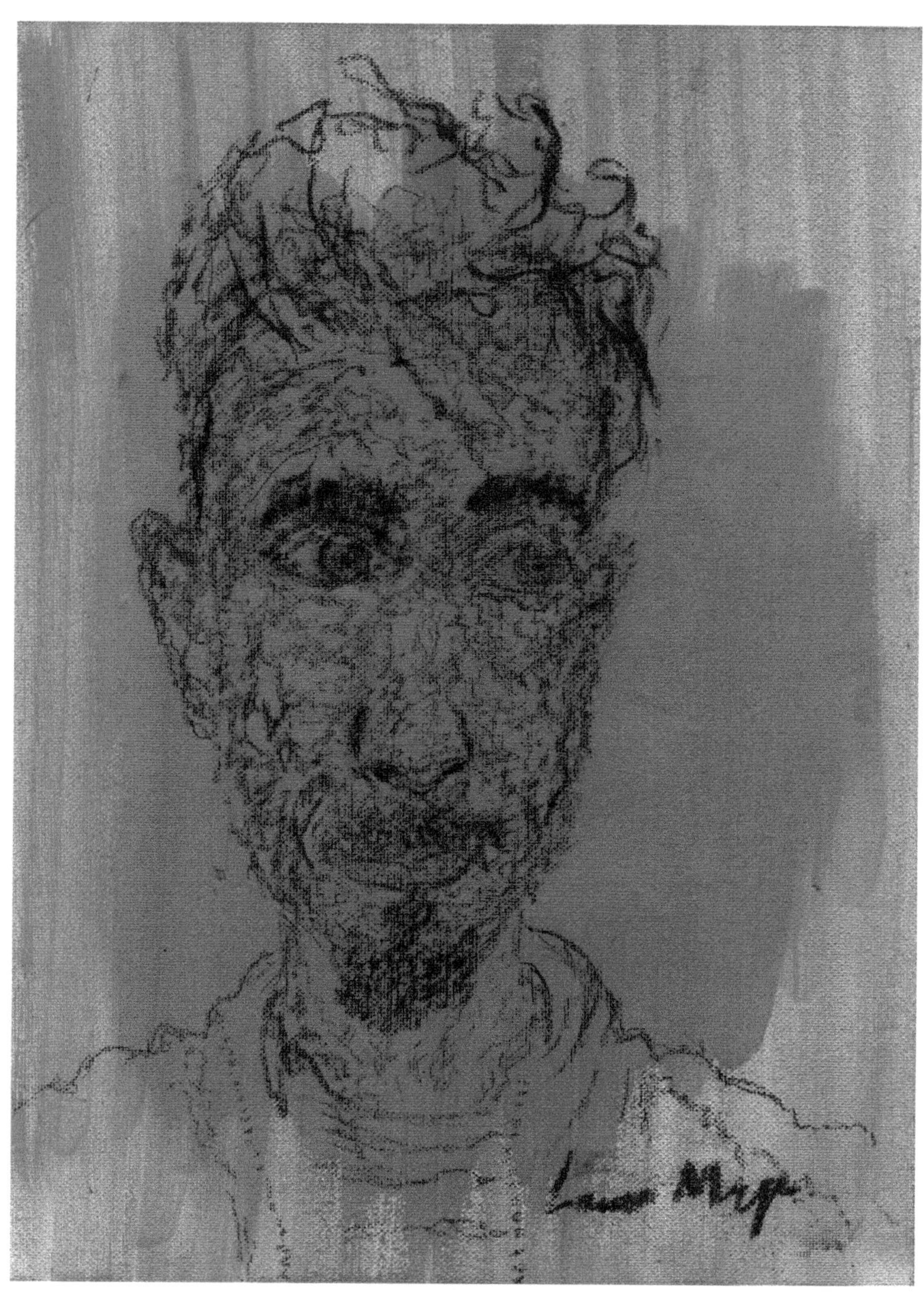

Canvas Portrait A
A charcoal poprtrait on an acrylic splodge of colour on canvas.
30.5 x 40.5 cm. 2018.

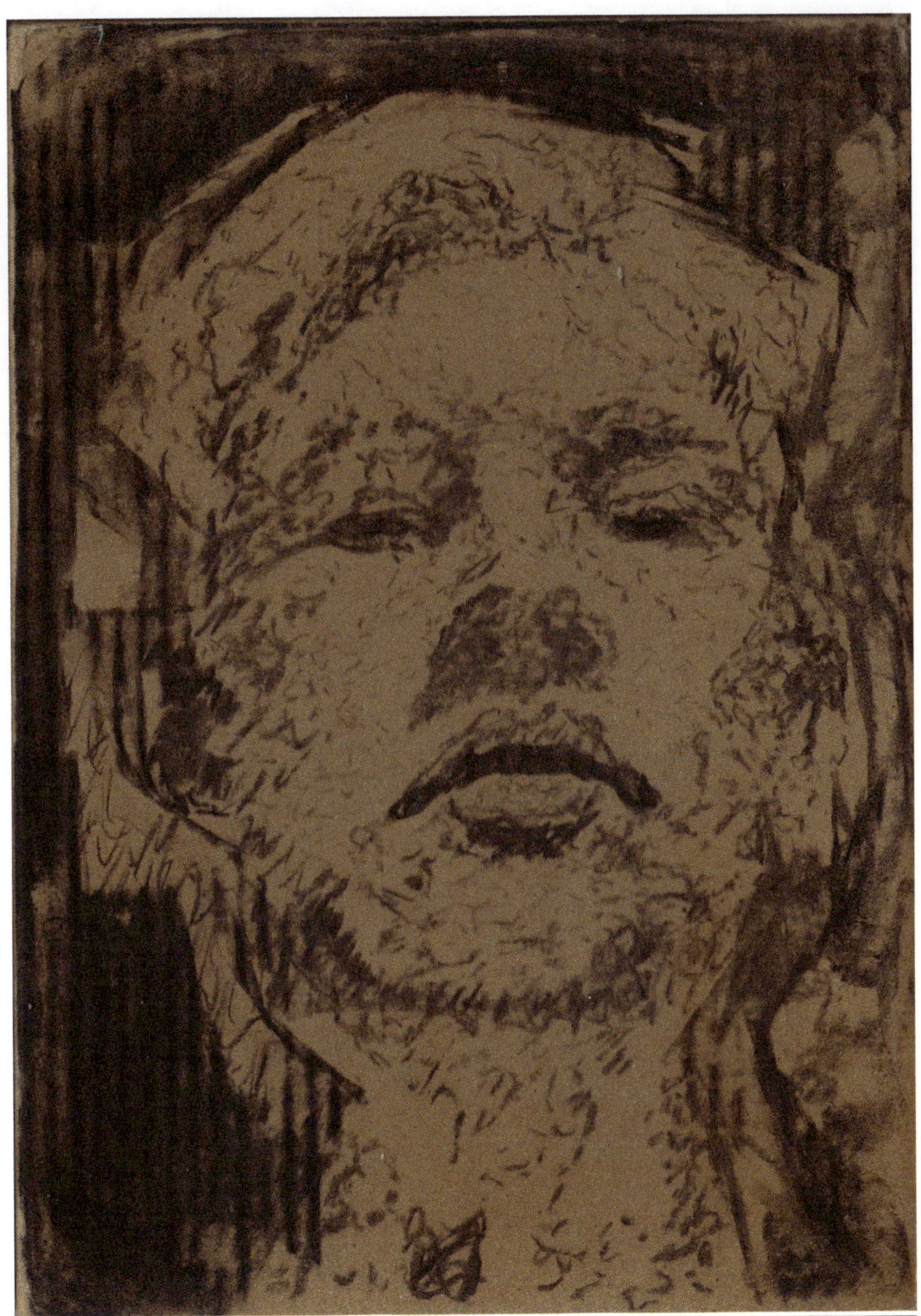

Cardigan
Charcoal on an intact cardboard box.
16 x 22 (...x 16) cm. 2018.

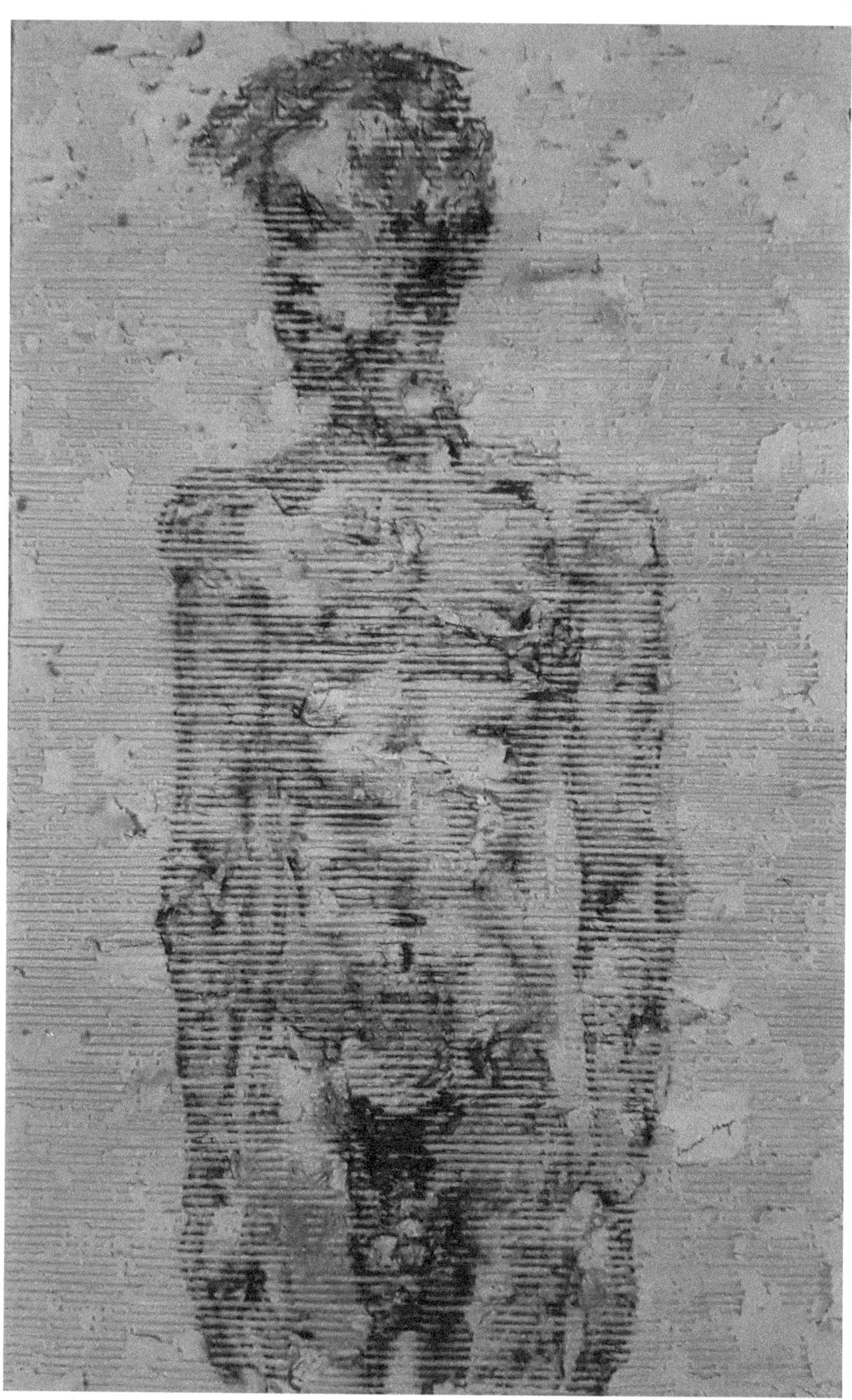

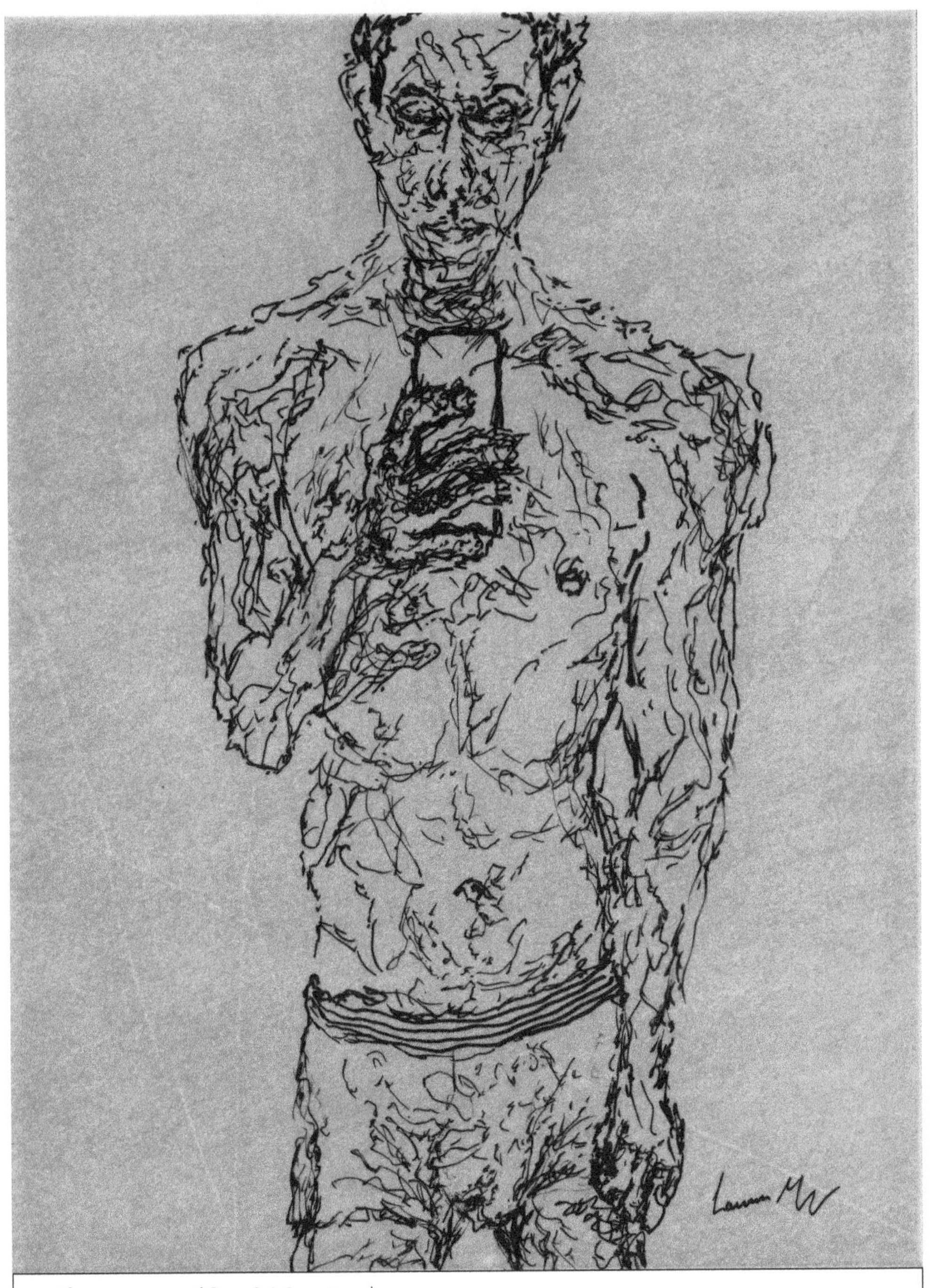

доброеутро *(Good Morning)*
Ink on recycled tile. 25 x 33.4 cm. 2019.

Opposite on page 44

Flare
Charcoal on deconstructed corrugated cardboard packaging.
31.7 x 56.4 cm (45 x 70.5 inc frame). 2018. My subject is a close friend. I found intrigue
with the idea of the 'Selfie' leading to and being captured, maybe superseded, by the art.

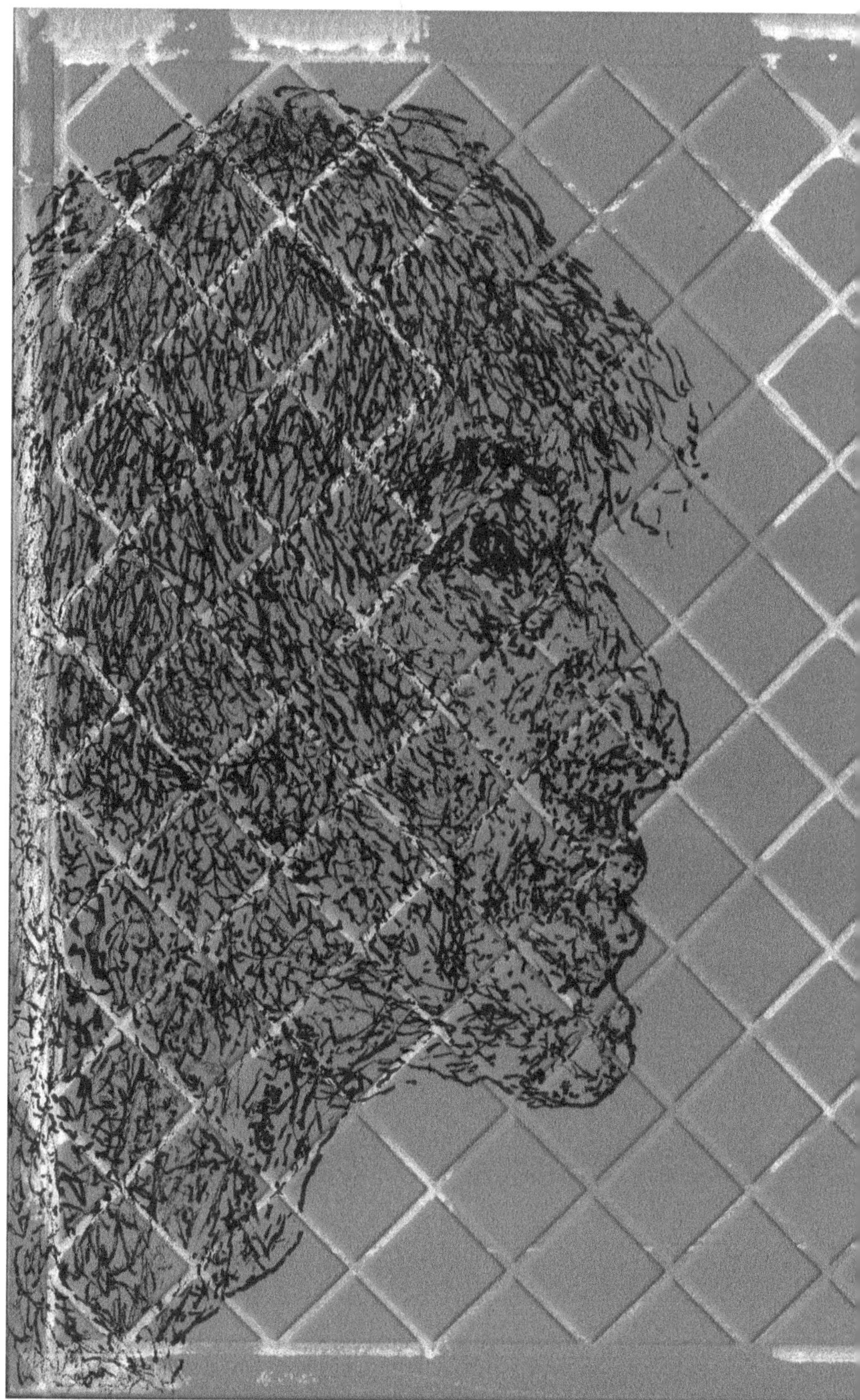

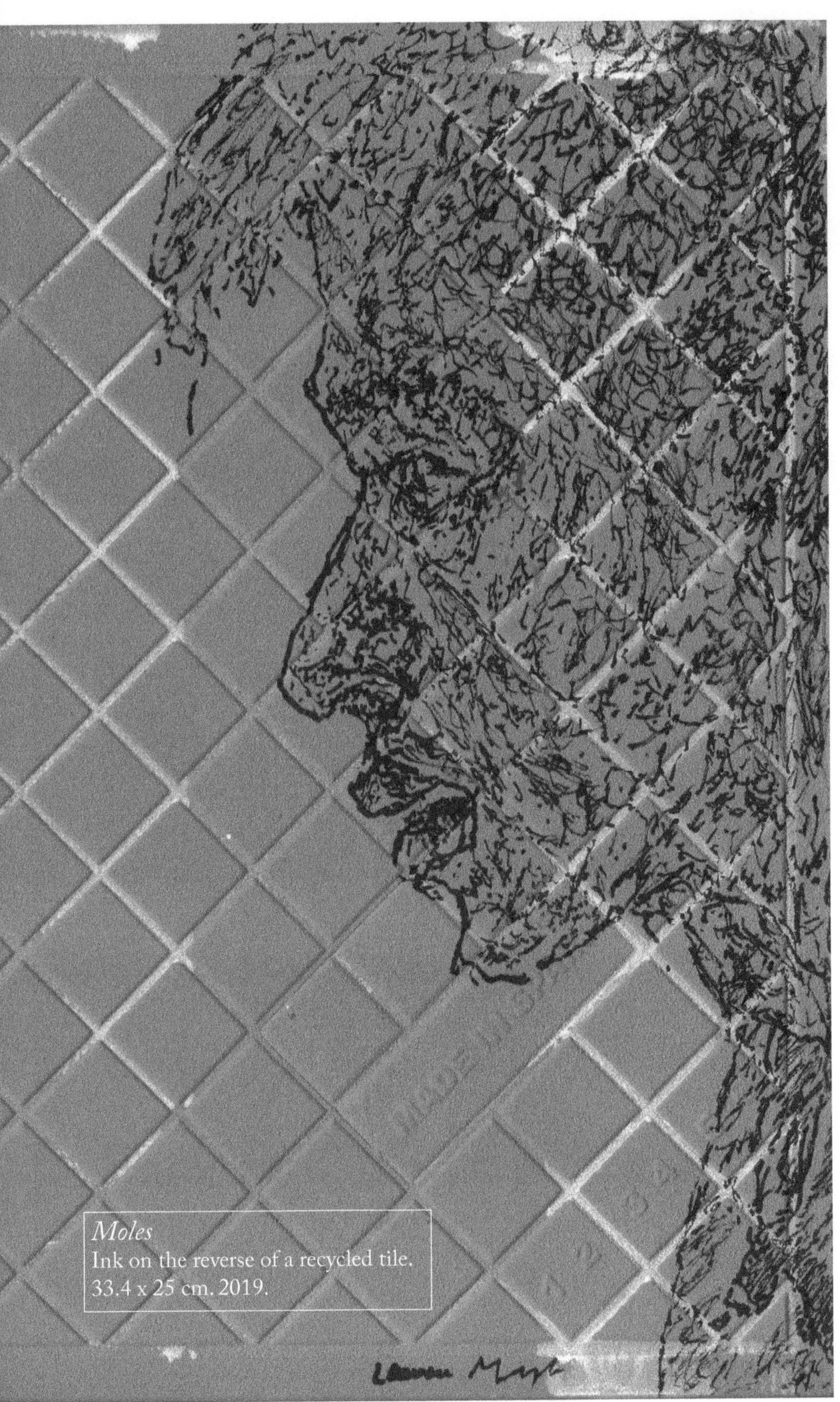

Moles
Ink on the reverse of a recycled tile.
33.4 x 25 cm. 2019.

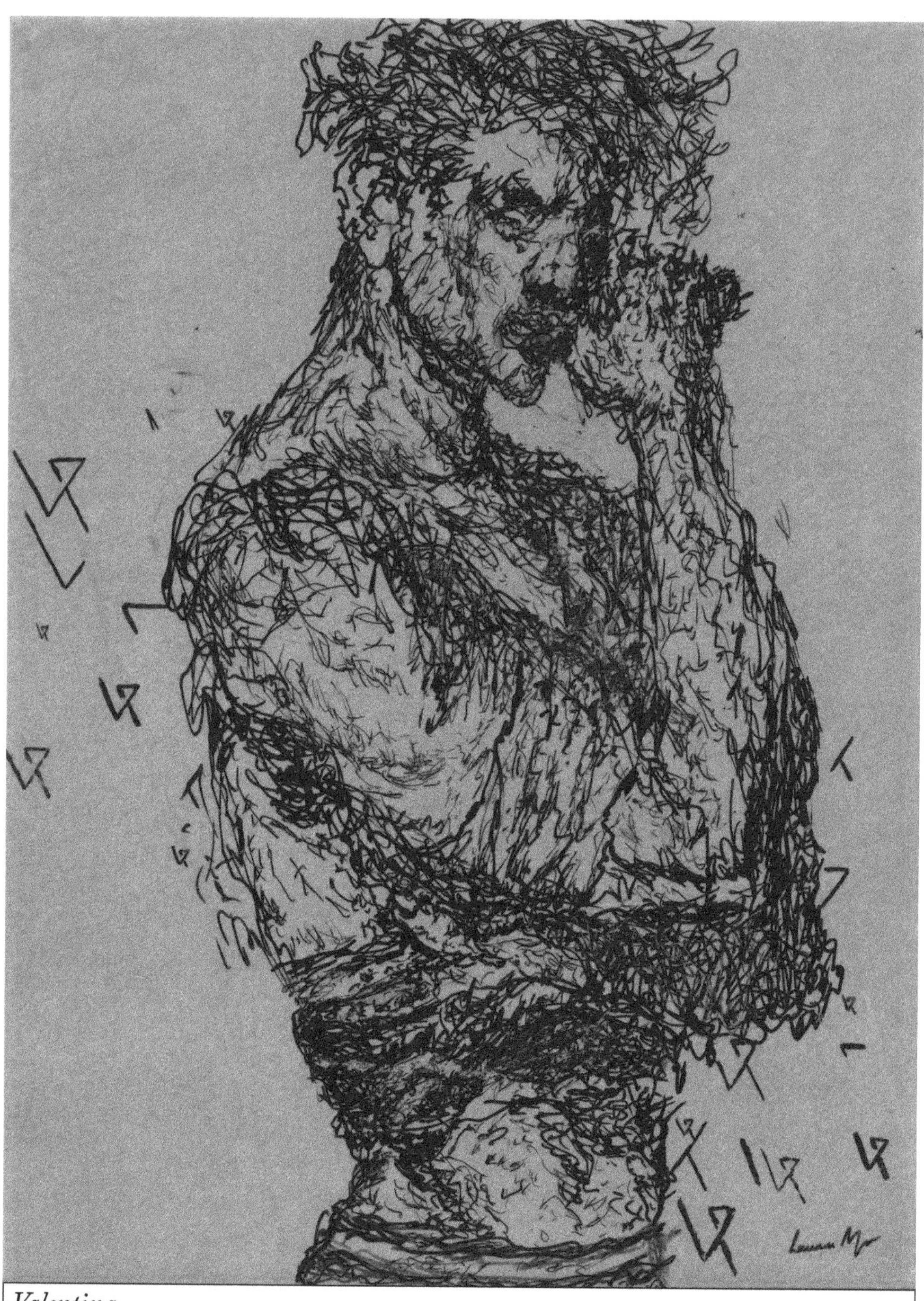

Valentina
Ink on a recycled tile. 25 x 33.4 cm. 2019.

On page 47:
Lighthouse
Charcoal on paper. 22.3 x 33.7 cm. 2017.

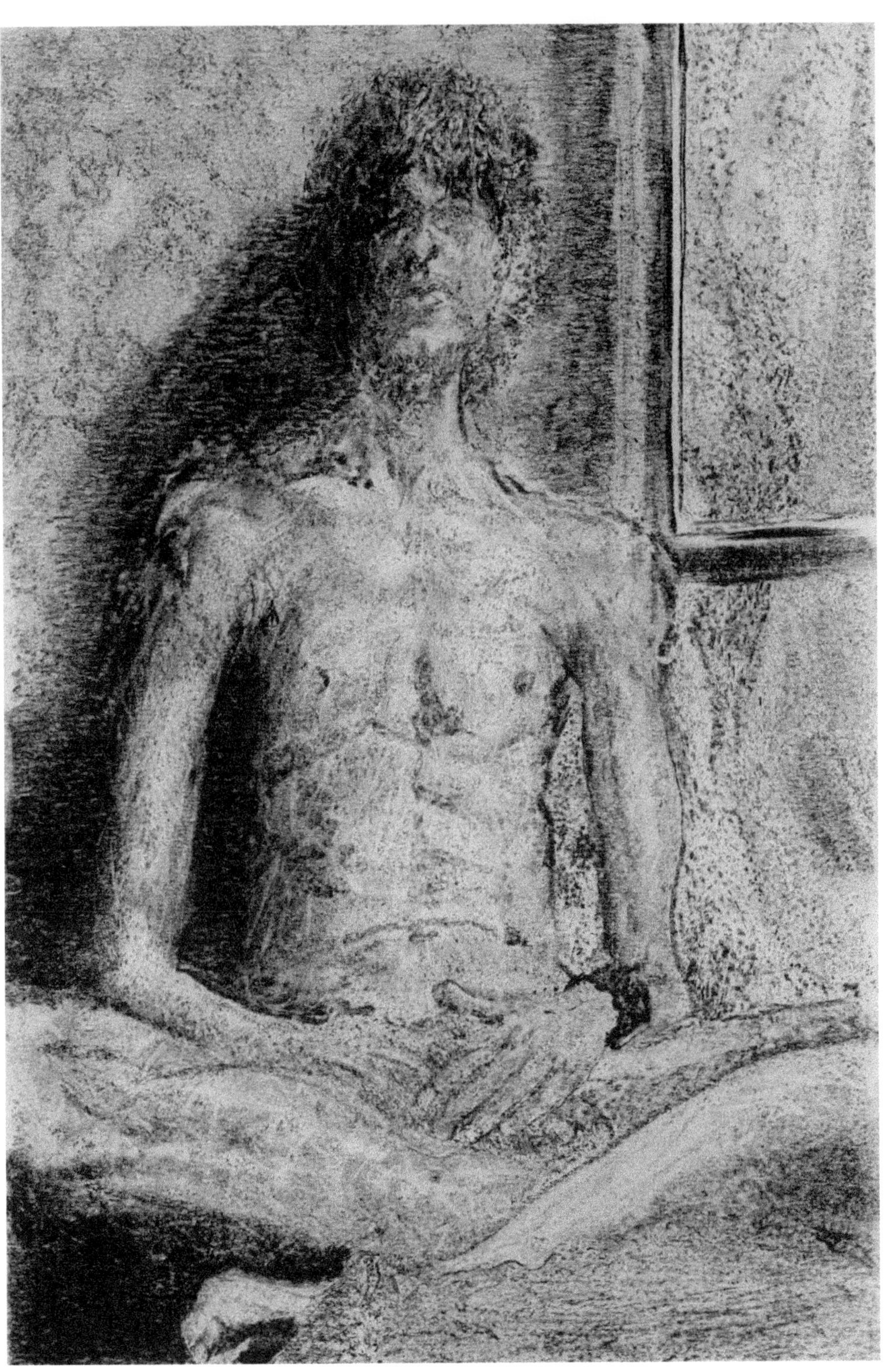

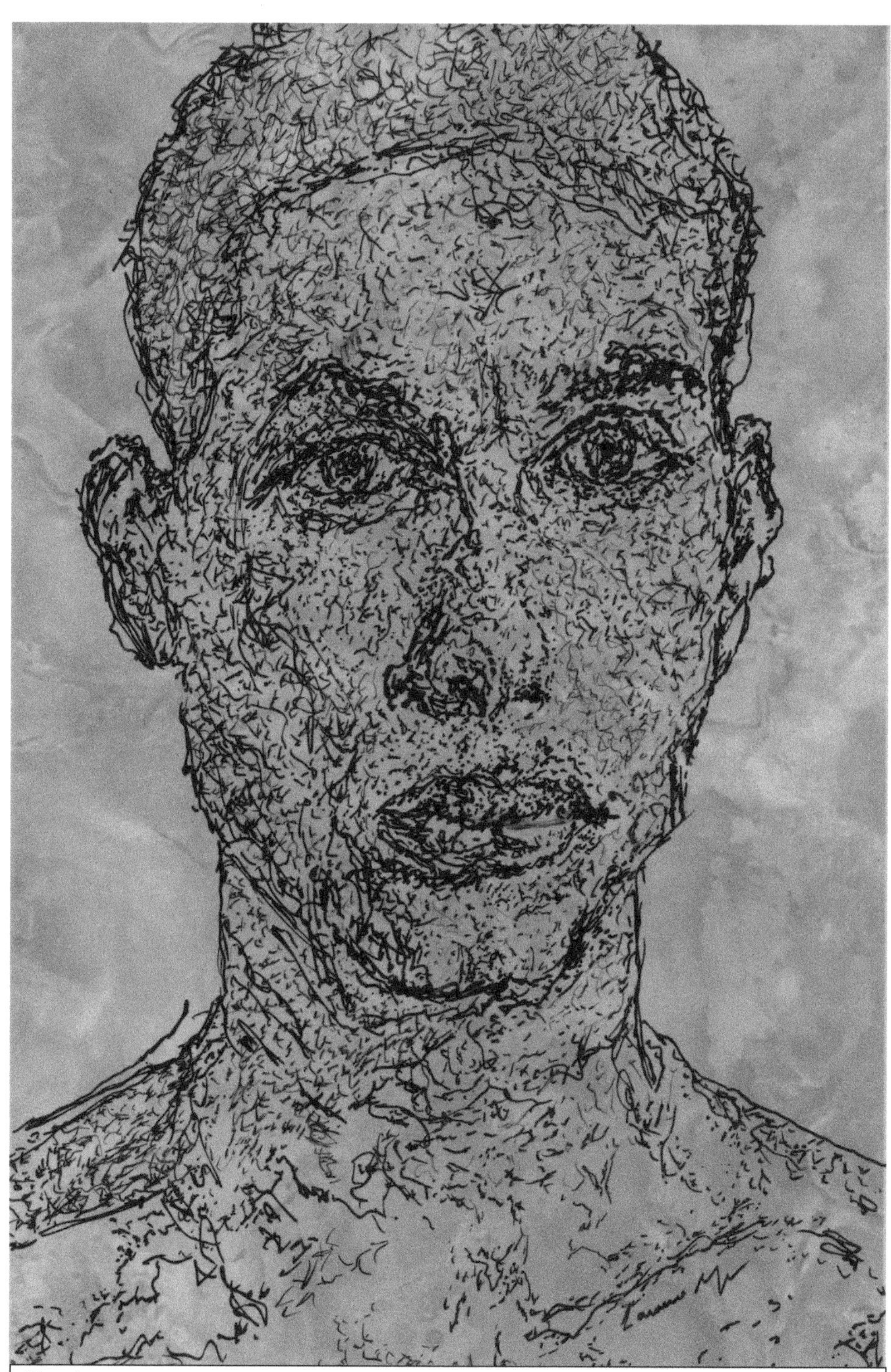

Sleepless
A portrait on a blue tile designed with a marbling effect.
20 x 31.6 cm 2019.

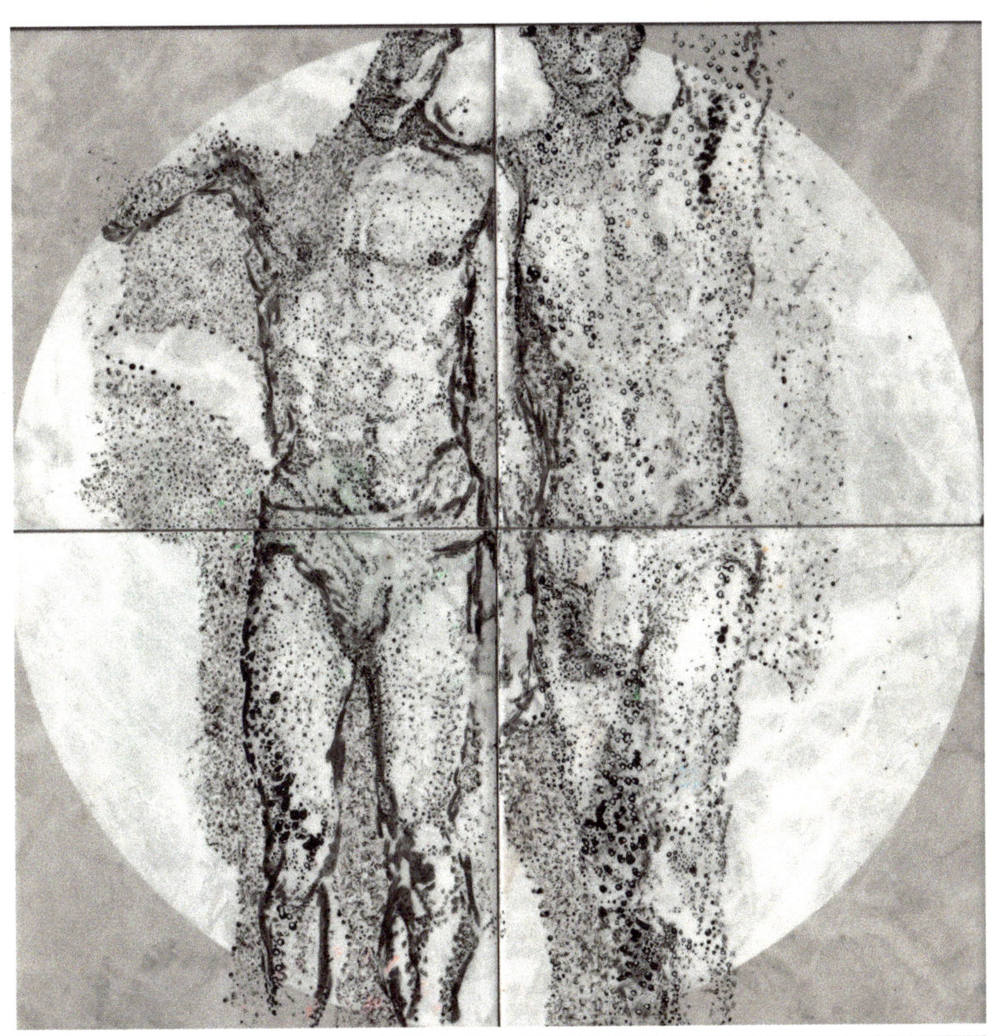

Seesaw
Ink over four recycled tiles.
29.7 x 29.7 cm. 2019.

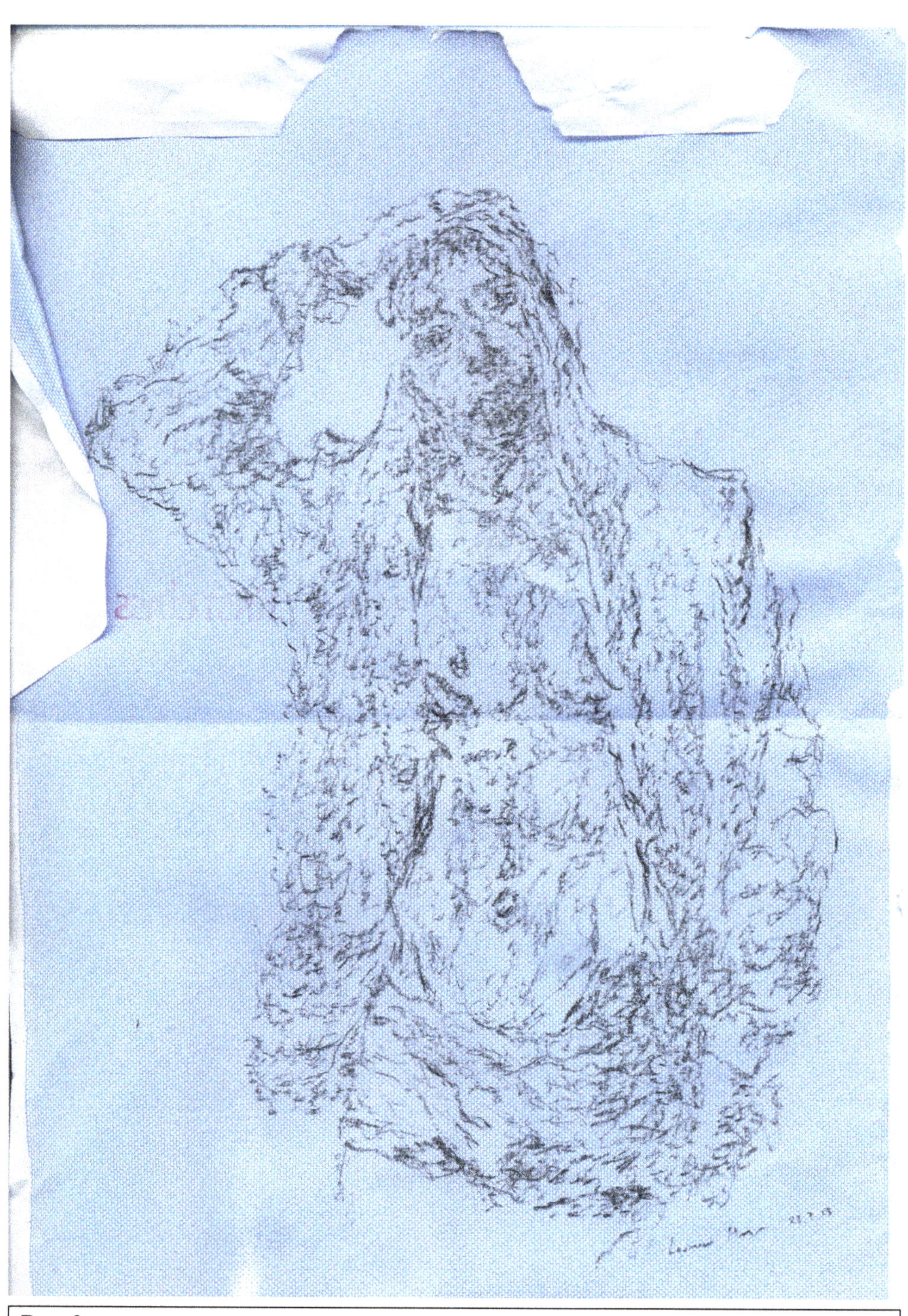

Proof
Charcoal on the inside of a used envelope.
Year 2018.

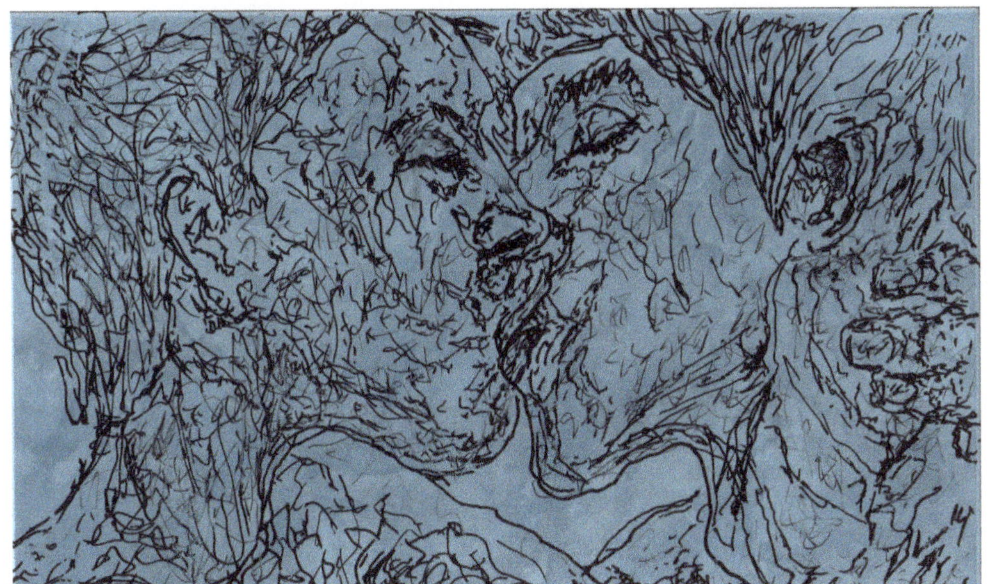

Venice Meeting Call
Ink on recycled tile. 31.6 x 20 cm. 2019.
This simple piece on the blue marbling designed tile I feel affords a surprisingly wonderful depth.

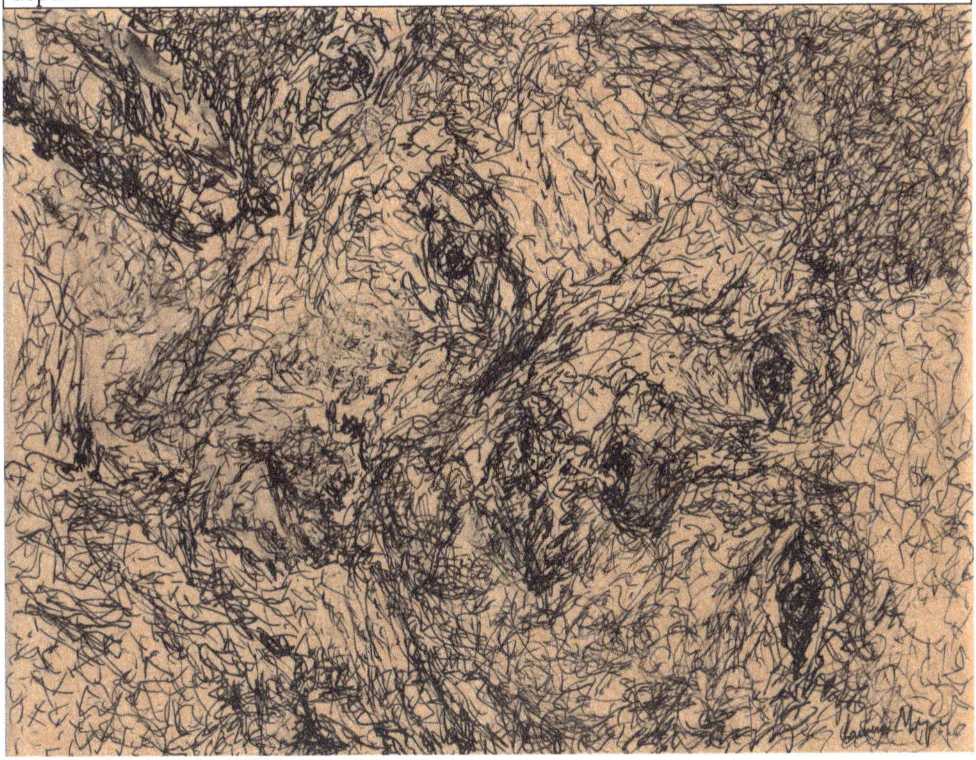

Not Everything Was Better In The Past
Ink on recycled tile. 33.4 x 25 cm. 2019.

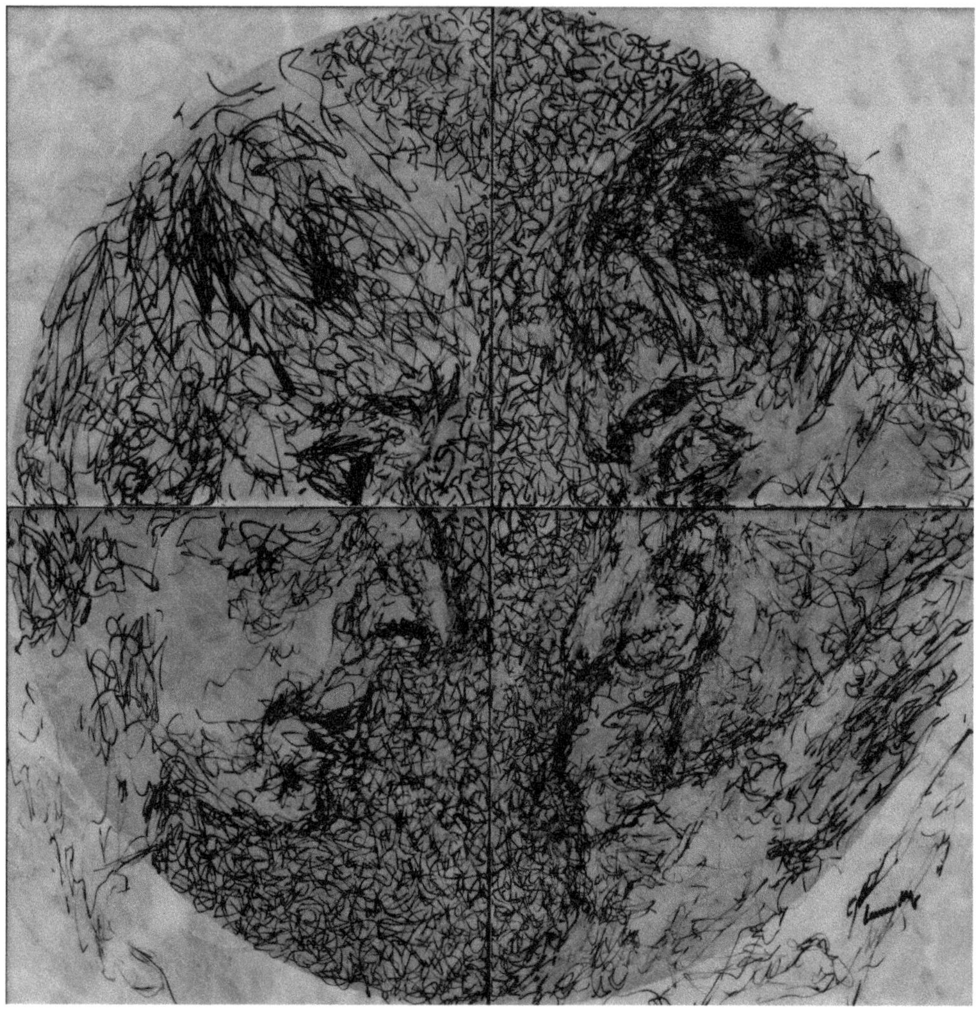

Above: *Tend*
Ink over four recycled tiles.
29.7 x 29.7 cm 2019.

Top page 53: *Balance*
Ink over four recycled tiles.
29.7 x 29.7 cm. 2020.

Page 53 below left: *Benji*
Ink on the patterned reverse of a broken tile.
24.8 x 28.6 cm. 2019.

Page 53 below right: *Black Winds*
Ink on recycled tile.
19.7 x 24.7 cm.2019.

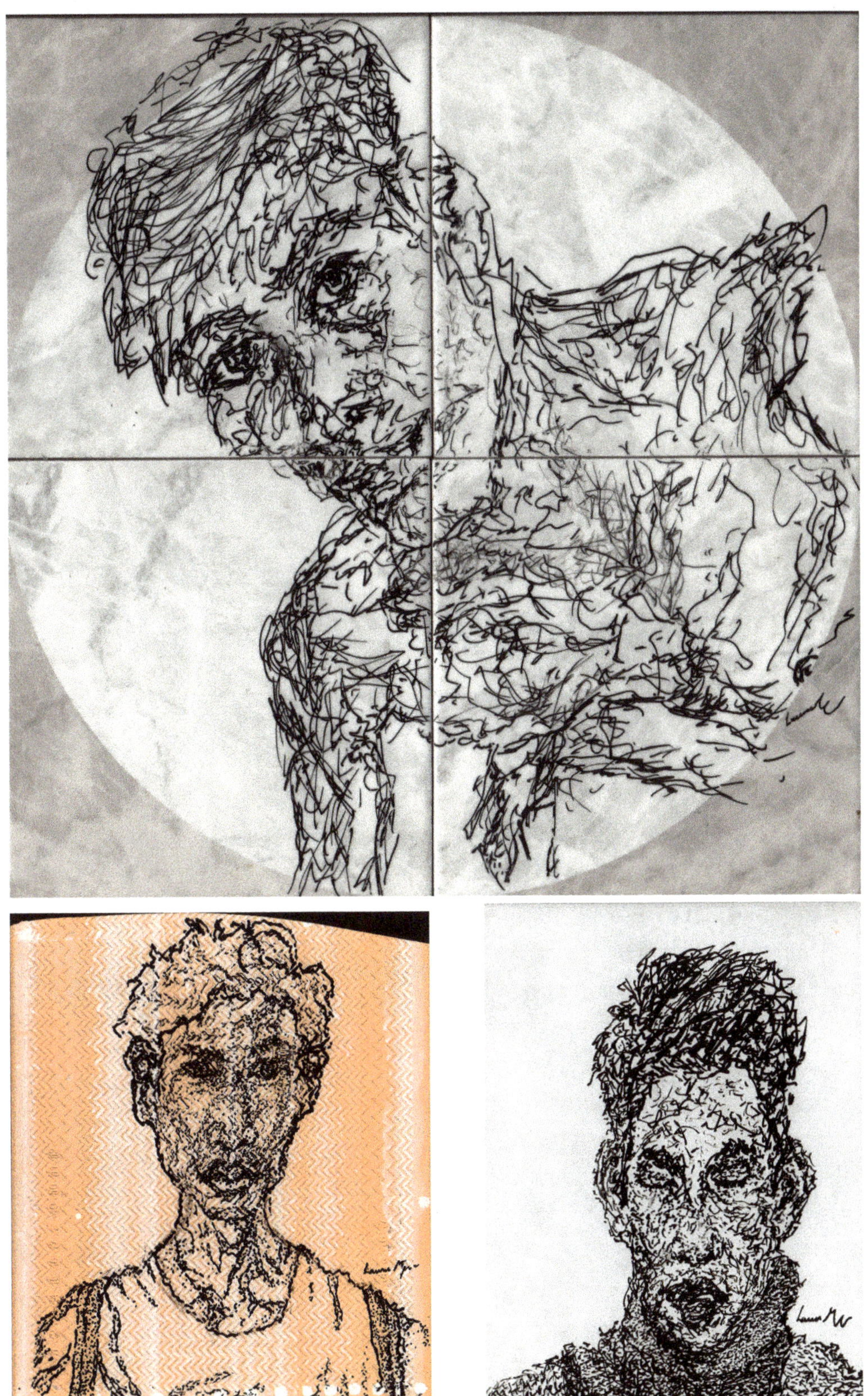

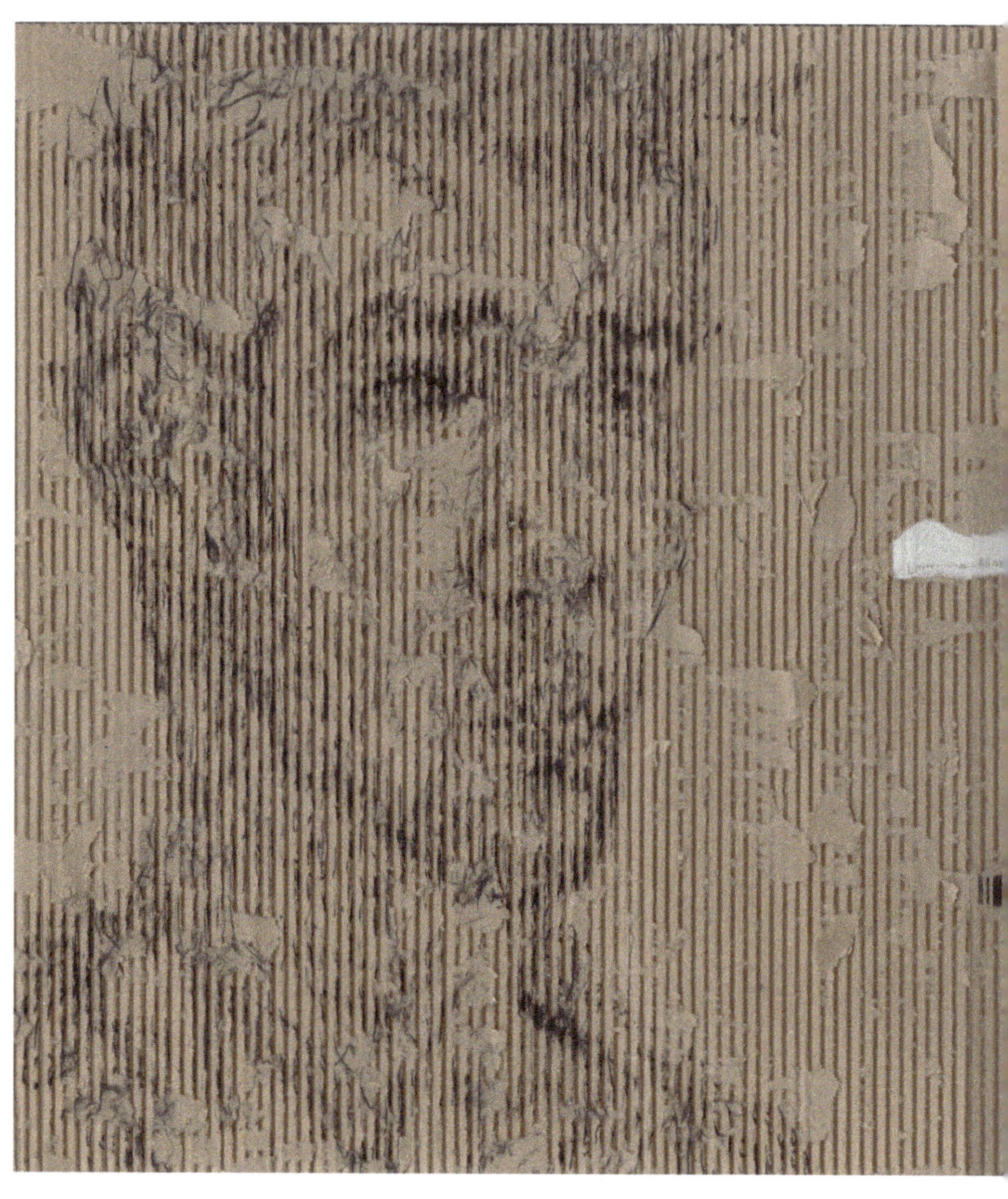

Unnamed Tick
Charcoal recycled cardboard packaging.
52.6 x 28.9 cm. 2020.

The image lays on deconstructed corrugation of the cardboard and 'Laurence Morgan' is visible on the remnants of a torn off address sticker. The dispatchers familiar curved tick/smile exists intact to the right side as does the perforated access strip.

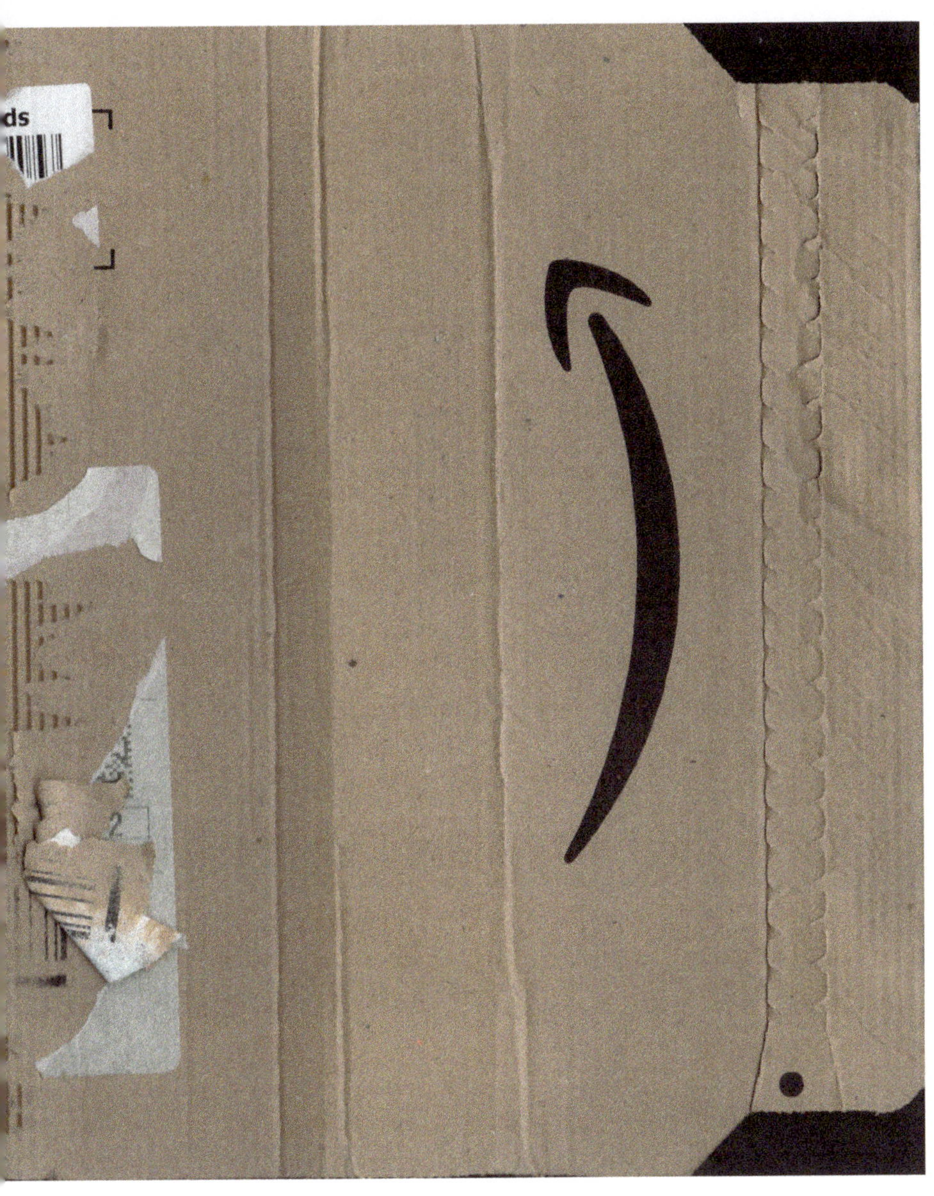

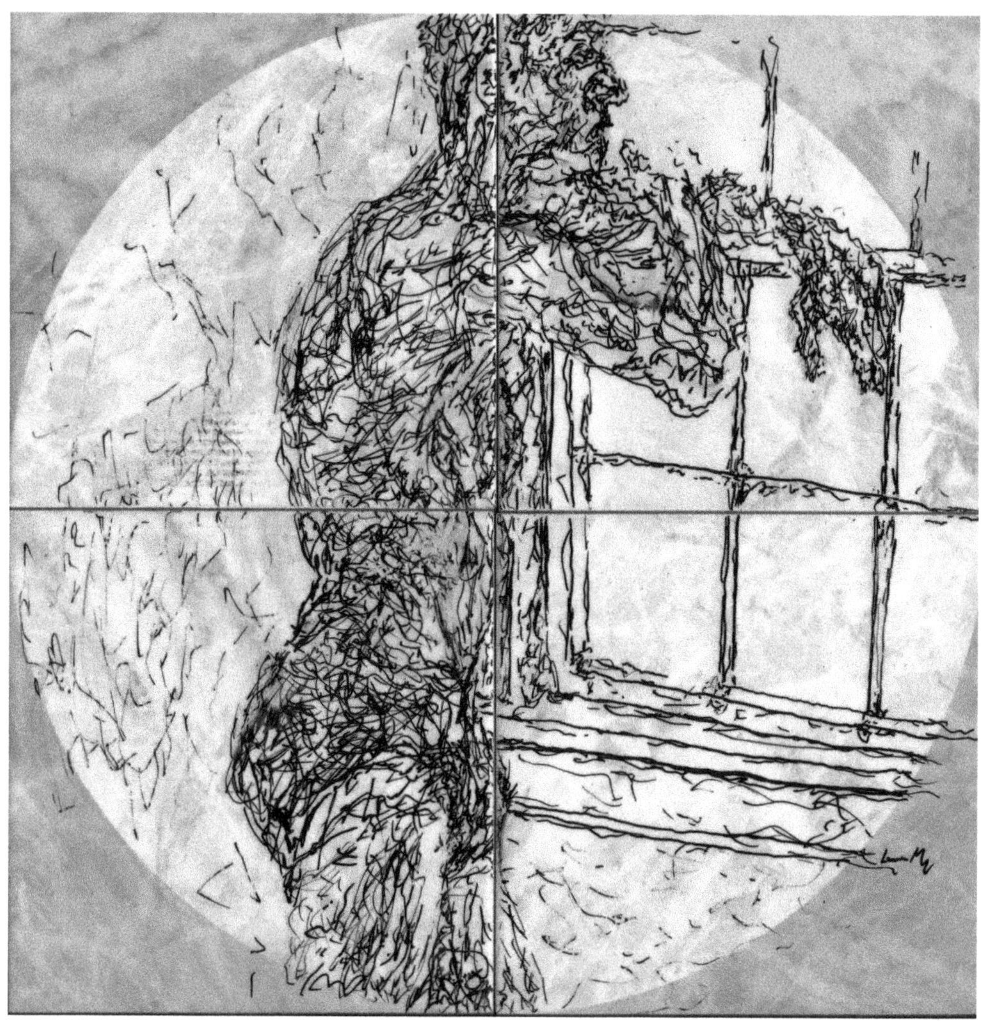

Above:
This Morning's Expresion
Ink over four recycled tiles.
29.7 x 29.7 cm. 2021.

On page 57 opposite:
Bowtie
Ink over four recycled tiles.
29.7 x 29.7 cm. 2021.

Fitted Sheets
Graphite stick on paper.
21 x 29.7 cm. 2012 (Below left)

Alone In Paris
Charcoal on paper.
23 x 29 cm. 2012. (Below right.)

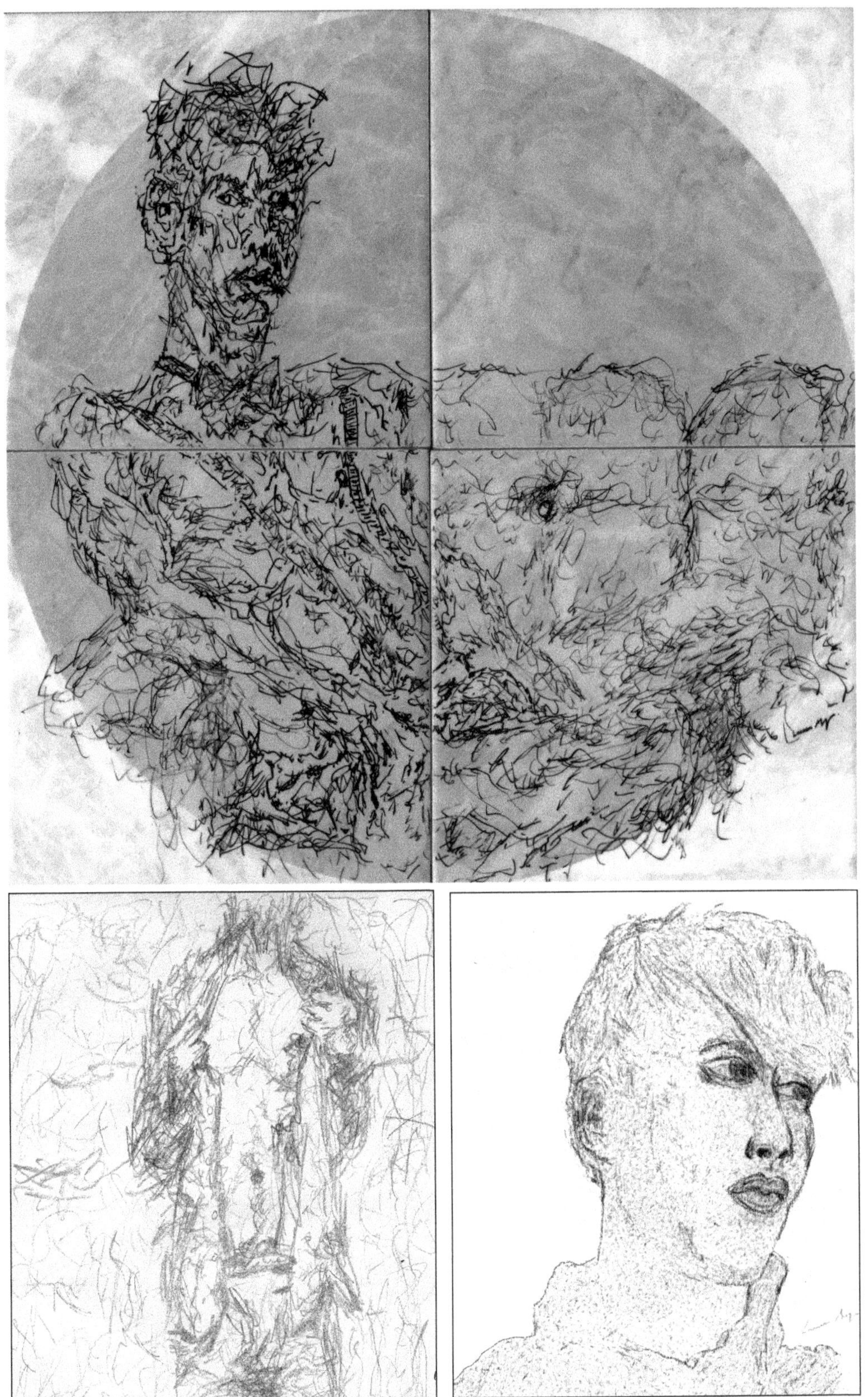

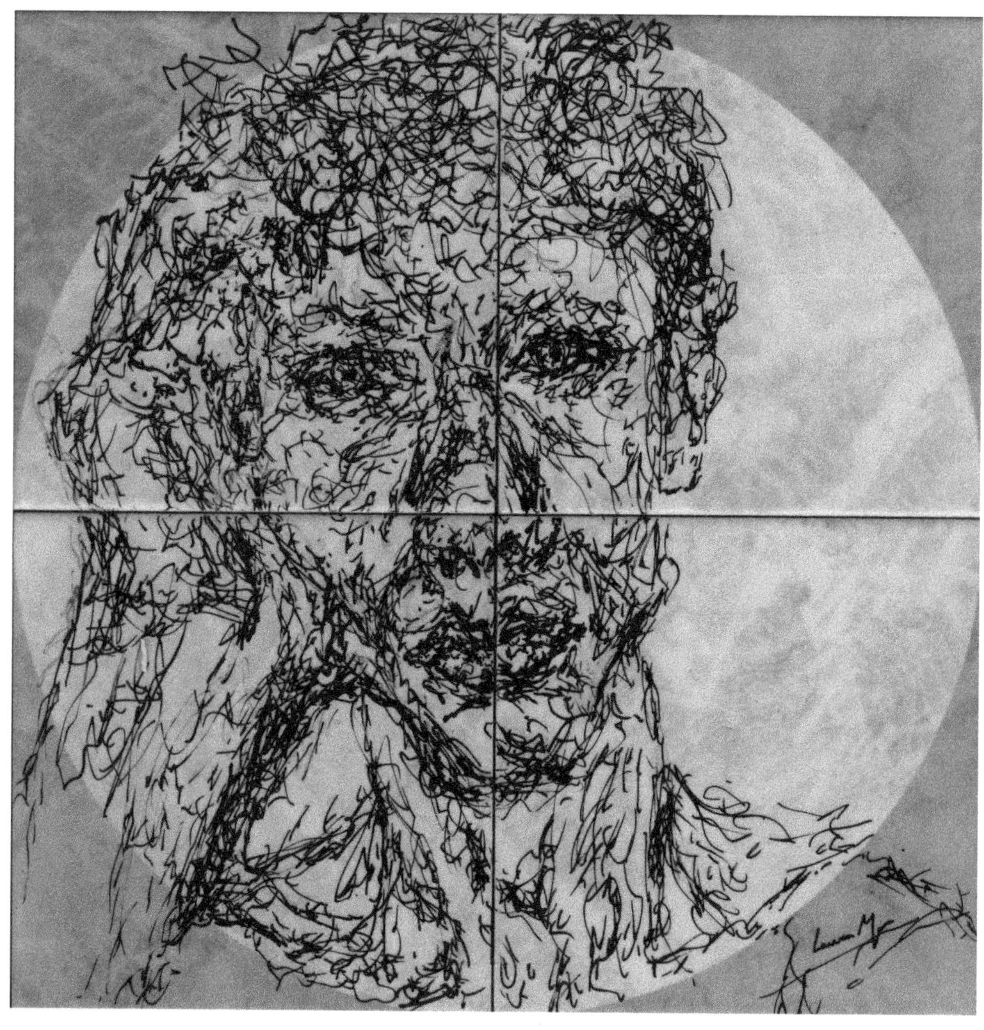

Faisal
Ink over 4 recycled tiles.
29.7 x 29.7 cm. 2019.

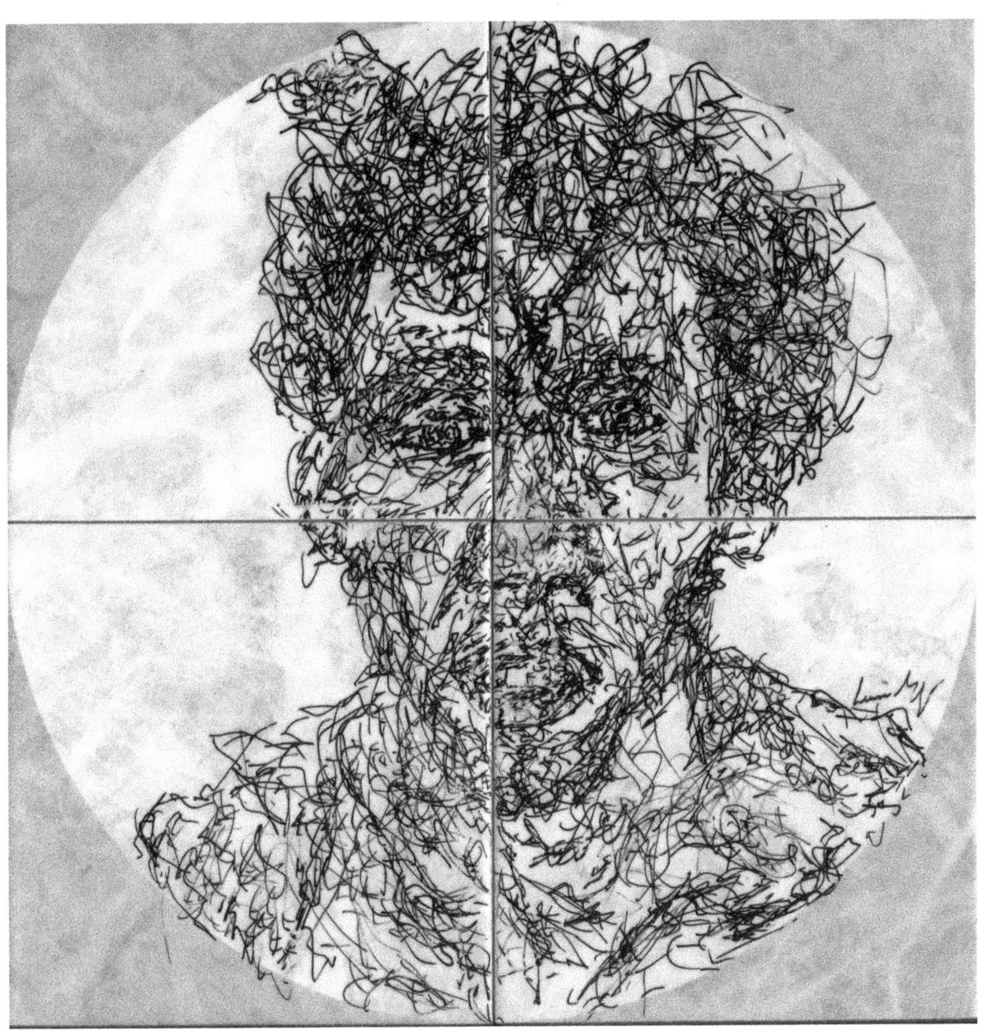

Dayron
Ink over 4 recycled tiles.
29.7 x 29.7 cm. 2020.
The tiles have an elliptical detailing/design that with four together creates a circle and creates what felt like a natural beautiful framing for images. This set have a darker designed area framing the circle.

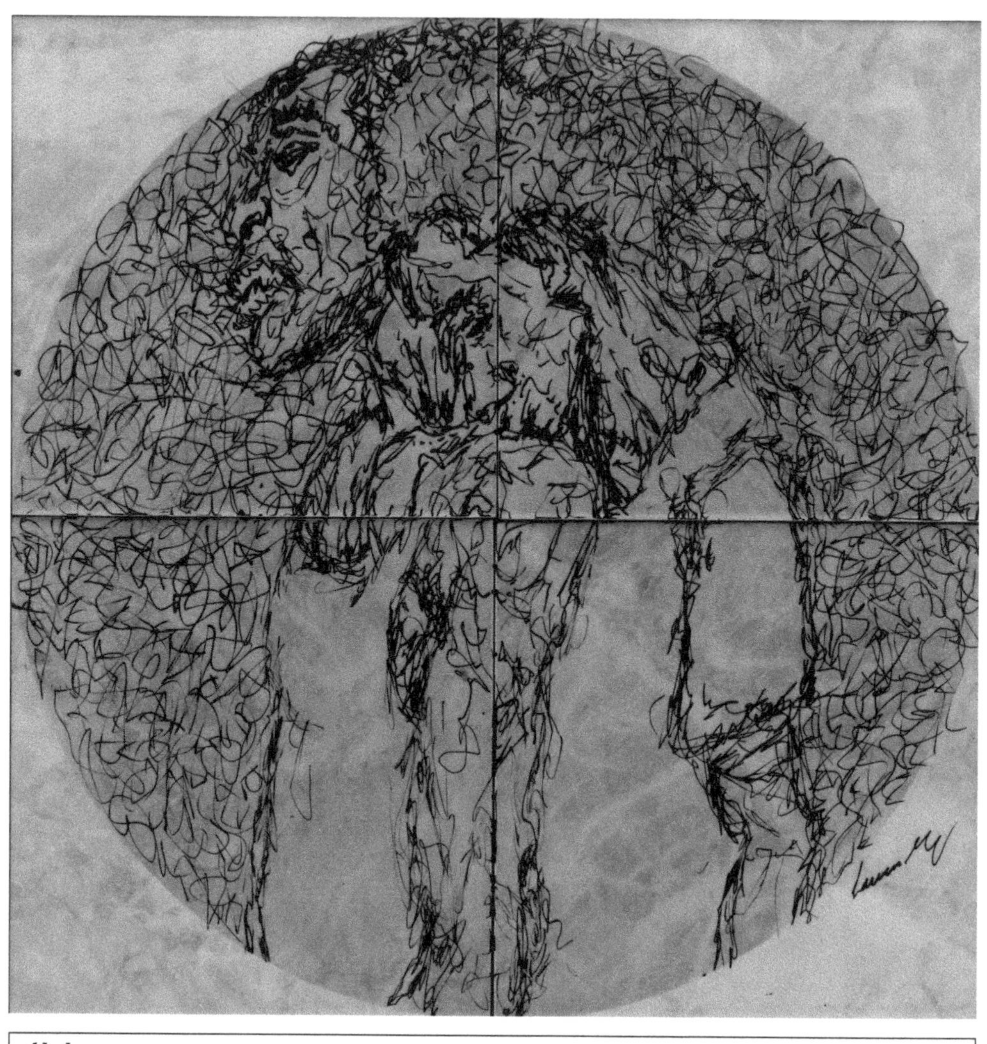

Abel
Ink over four recycled tiles.
29.7 x 29.7 cm. 2019.

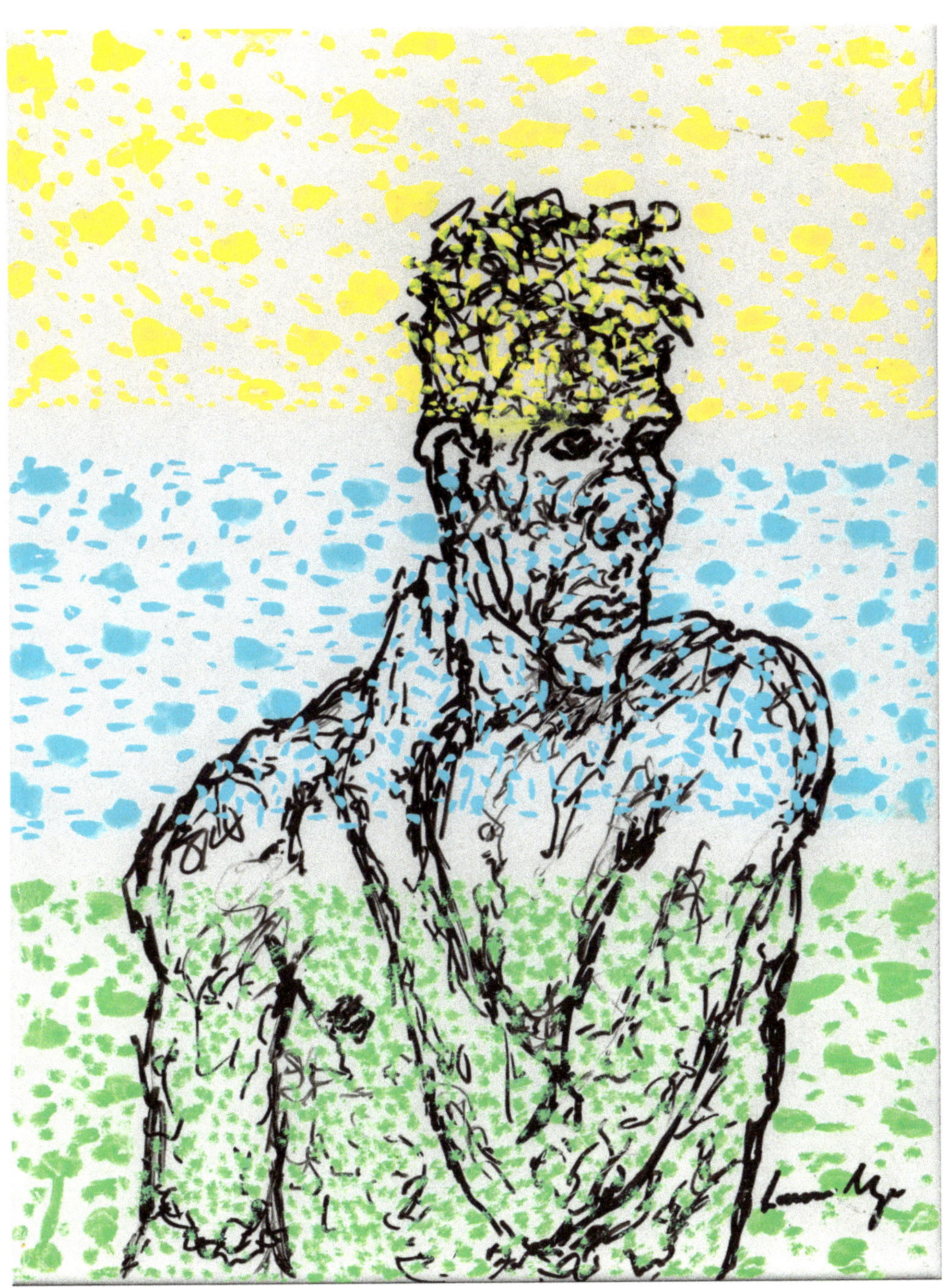

Bridges
Ink on recycled tile.
27.6 x 36 cm. 2019.

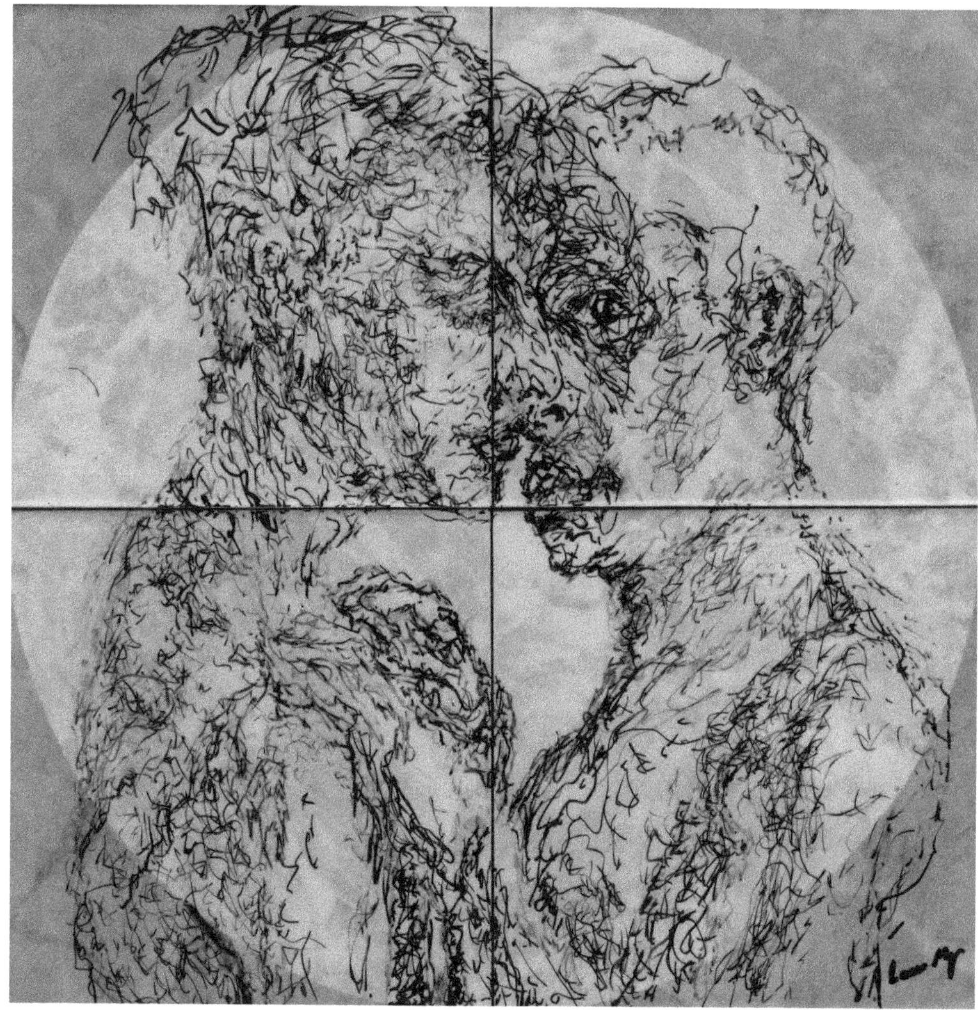

Words Unspoken
Ink over four recycled tiles.
29.7 x 29.7 cm. 2019.

On page 63.
Julio
Ink over four recycled tiles.
29.7 x 29.7 cm 2019.

Below Left:

Jamie
Charcoal on Canvas
40 x 30 cm

Below Right:

Postcard Portrait 05
Ink on card. 9 x 14 cm. 2021

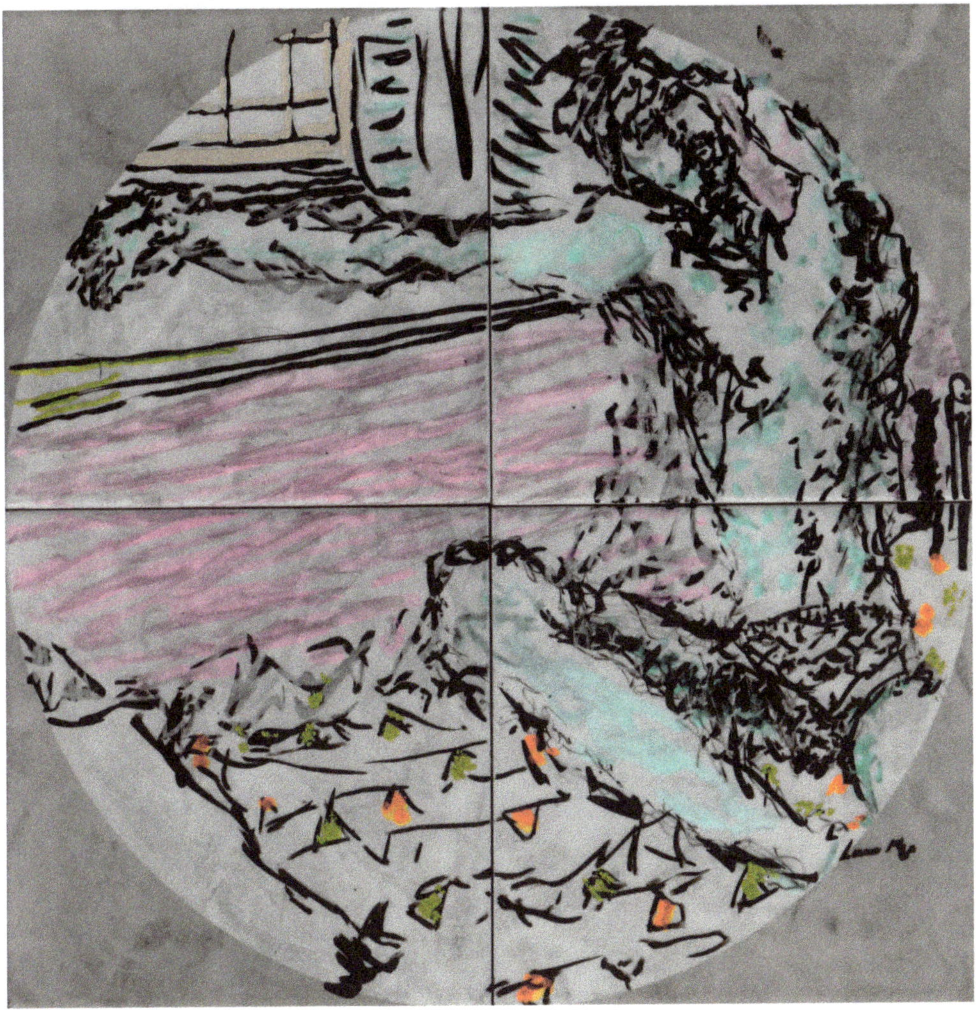

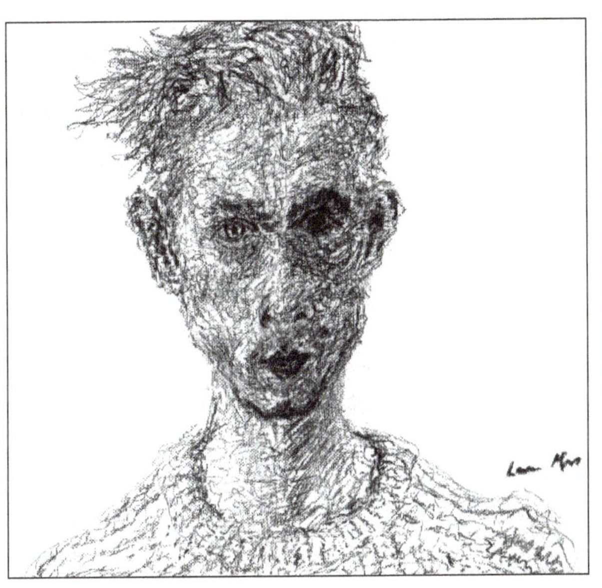
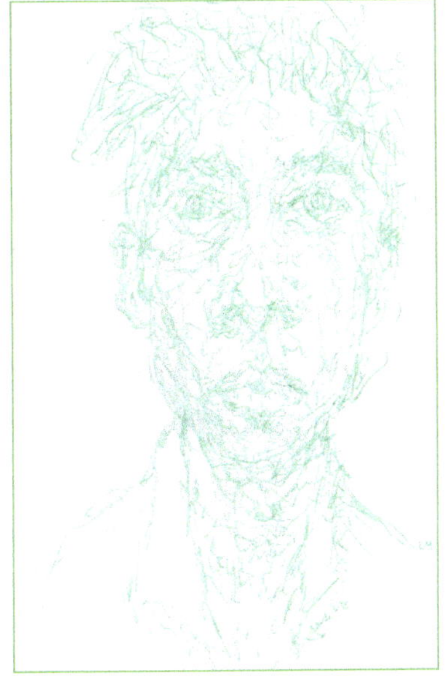

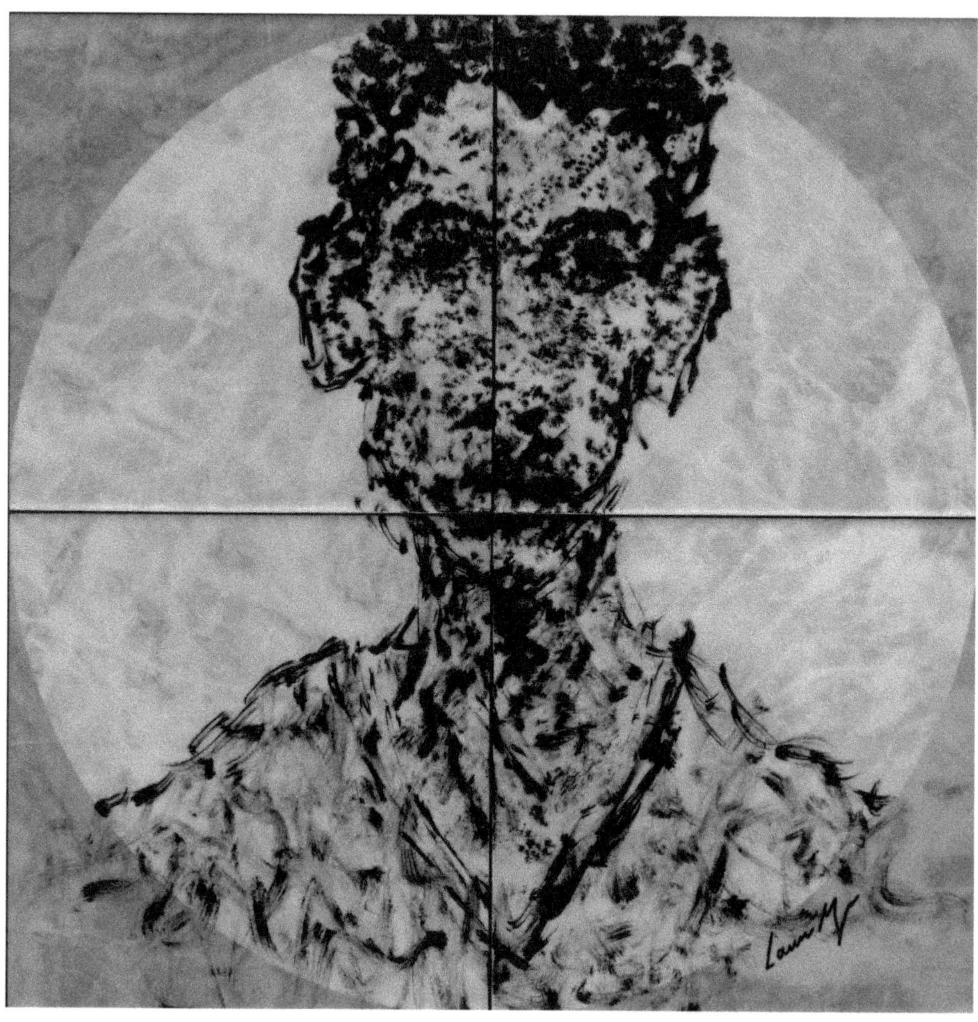

Above:
Knot
Ink over four recycled tiles.
29.7 x 29.7 cm. 2020.

Opposite:
Vampires
Ink on recycled tile.
20 x 31.6 cm. 2019.
A loose portrait on a blue tile designed with a marbling effect. Something about the intensity of those eyes led me to its title.

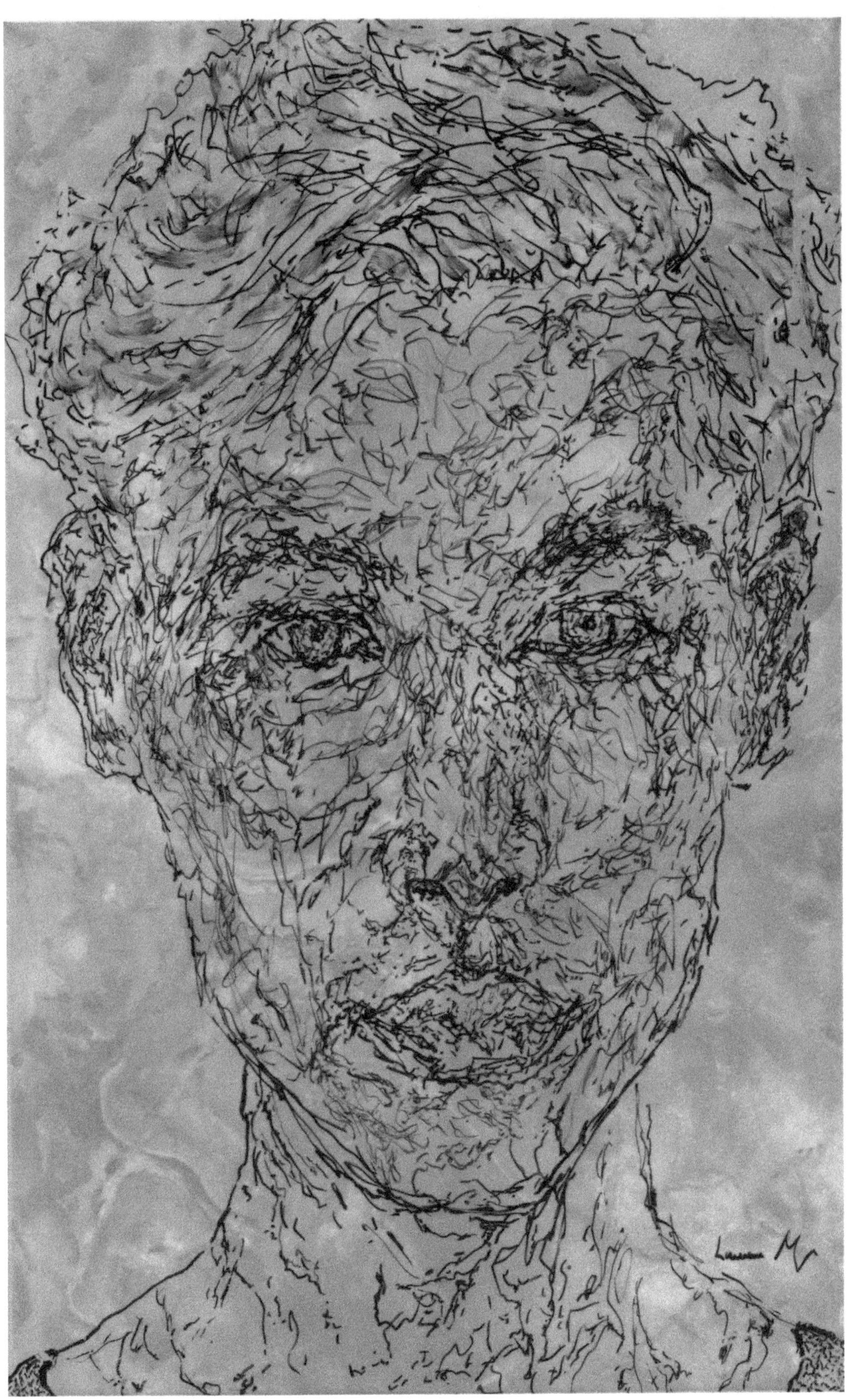

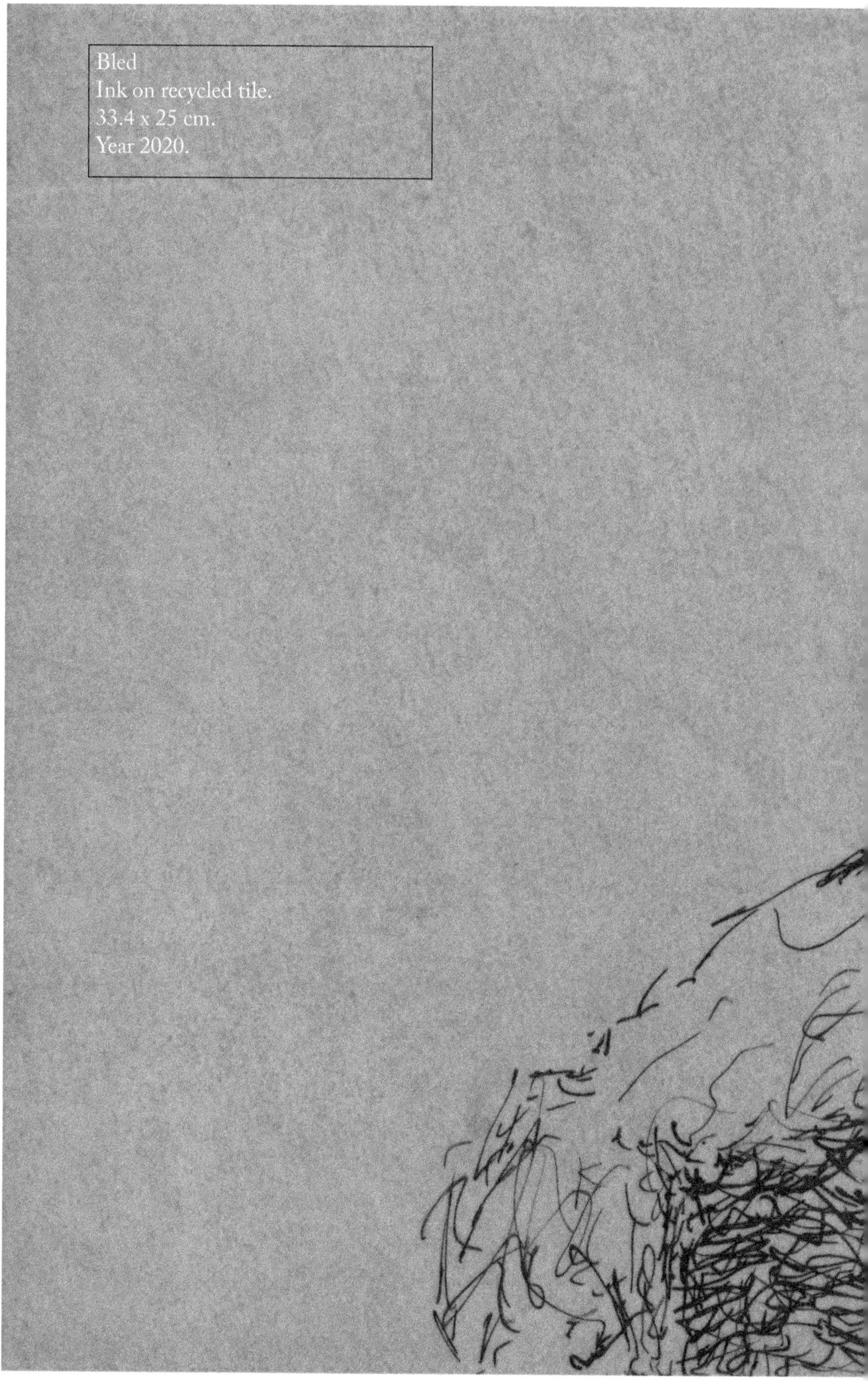

Bled
Ink on recycled tile.
33.4 x 25 cm.
Year 2020.

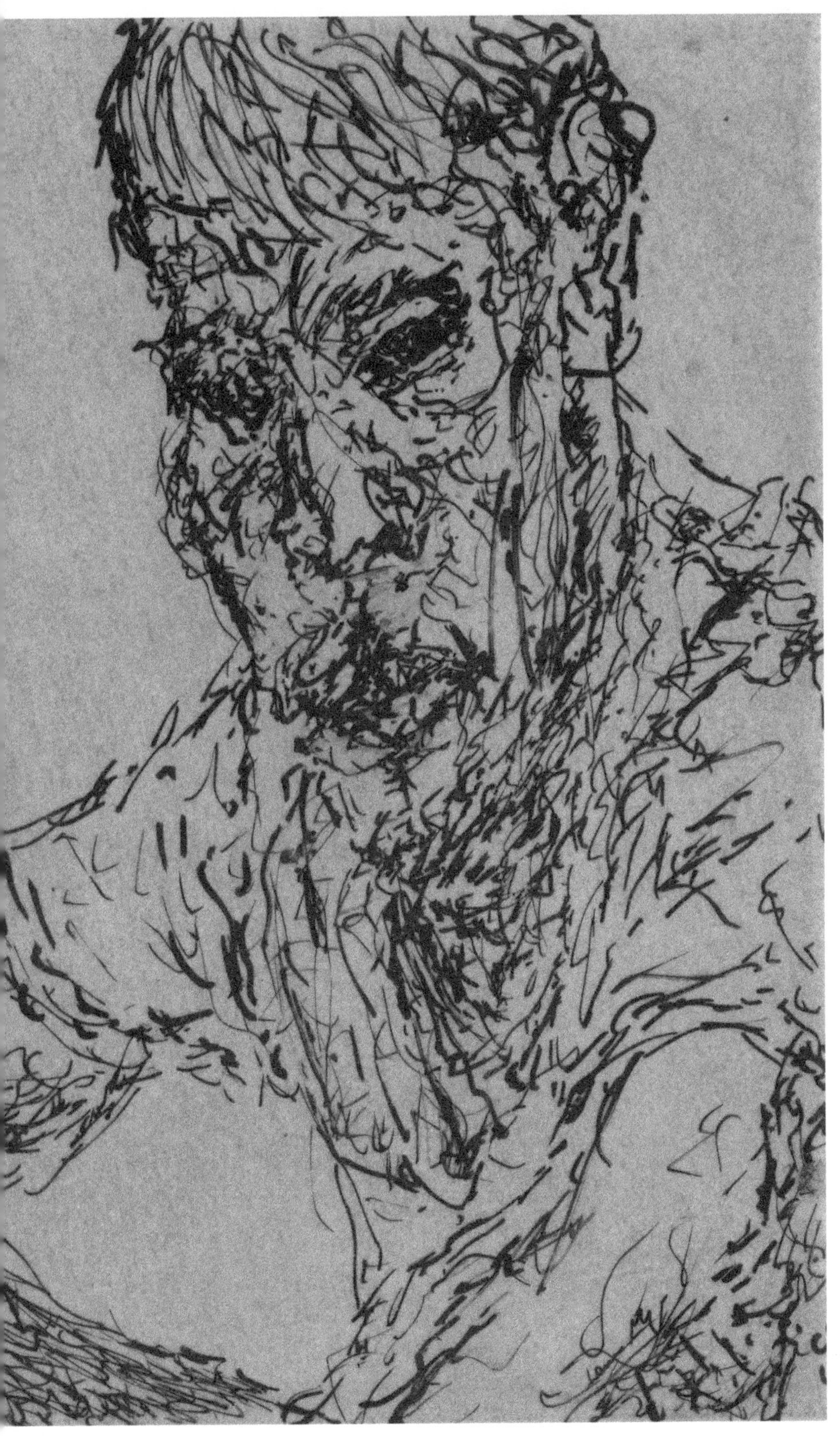

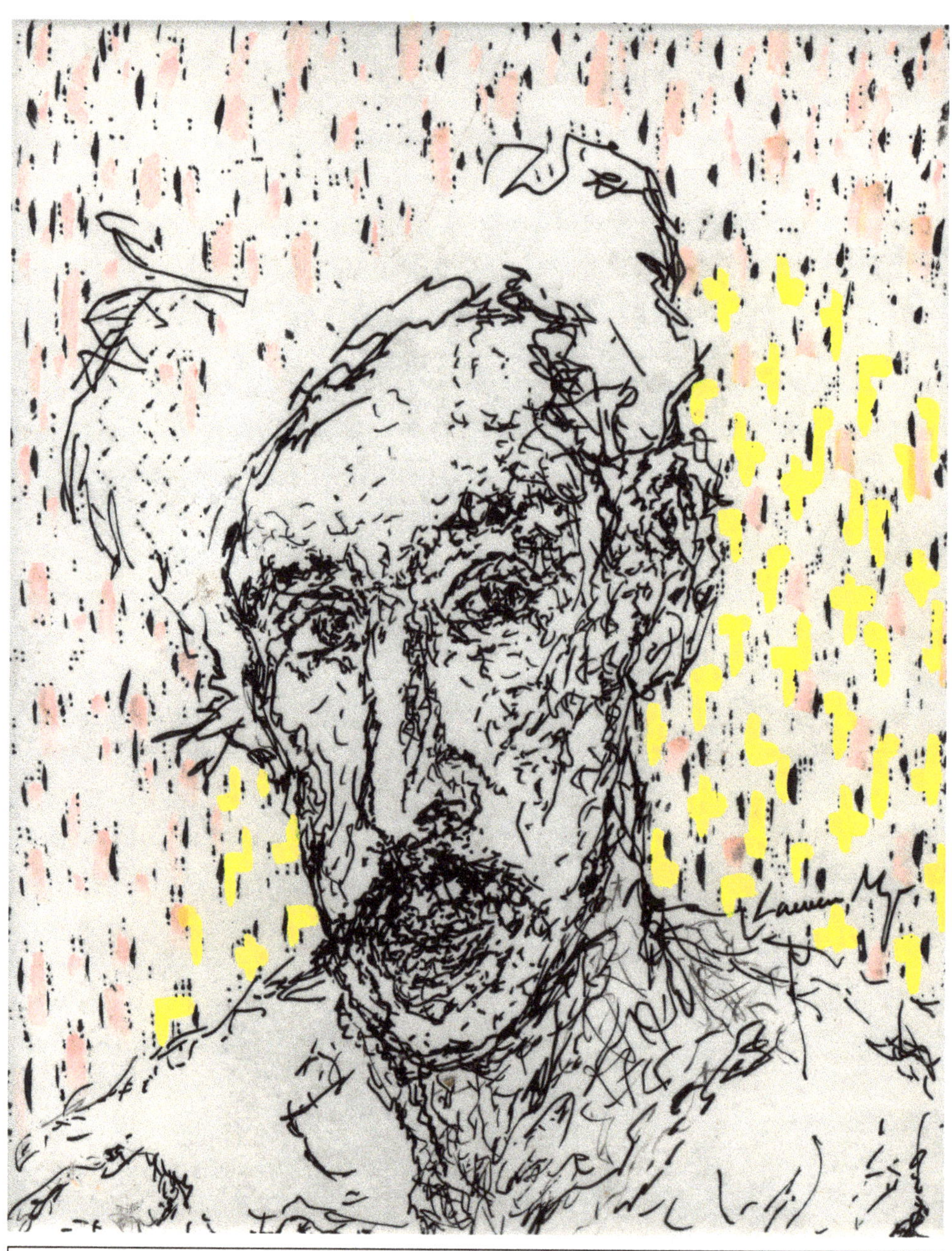

Chicago Blues
Ink on a recycled tile.
19.8 x 24.8 cm. 2019.

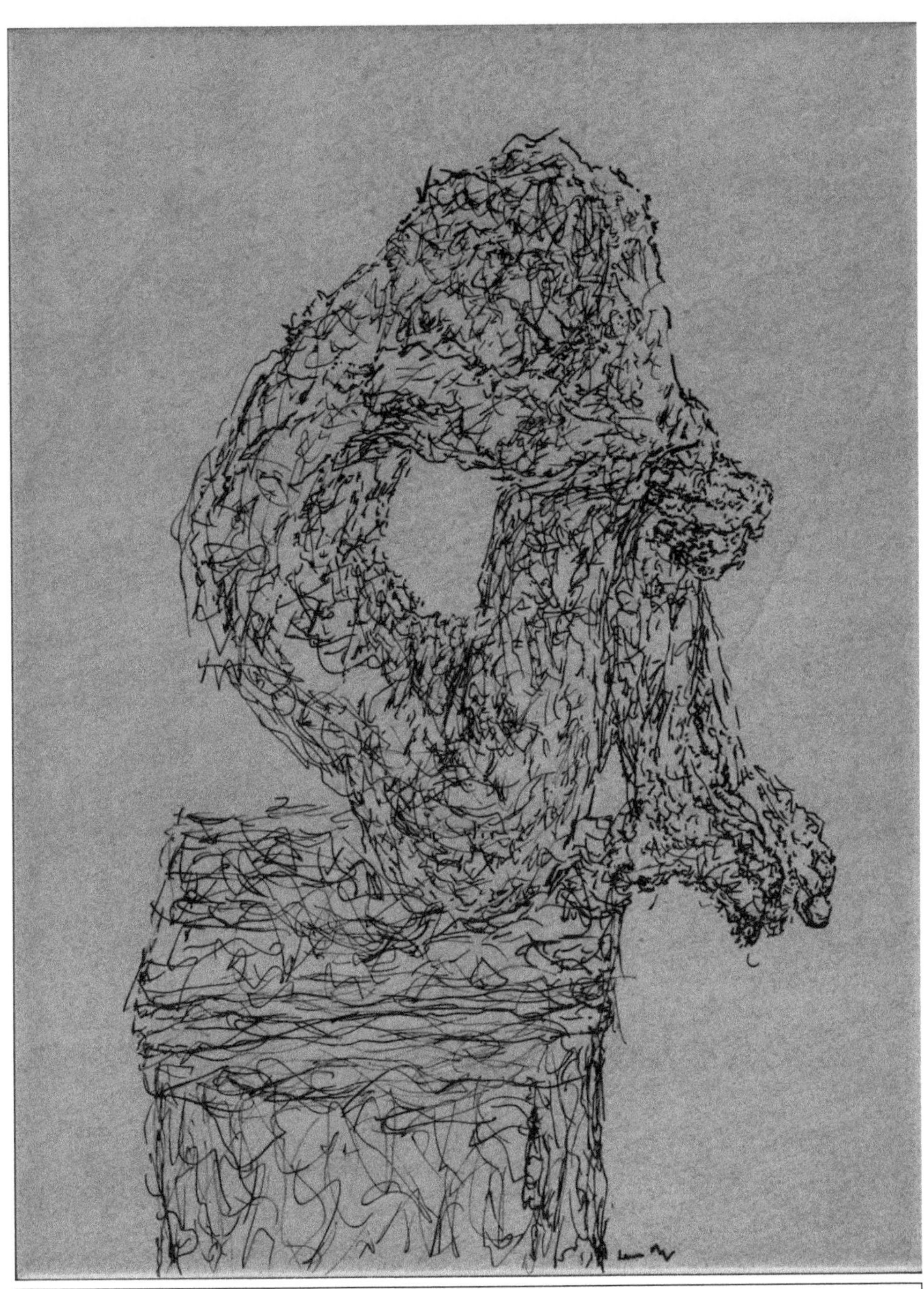

Colm
Ink on tile.
25 x 33.4 cm. 2021.

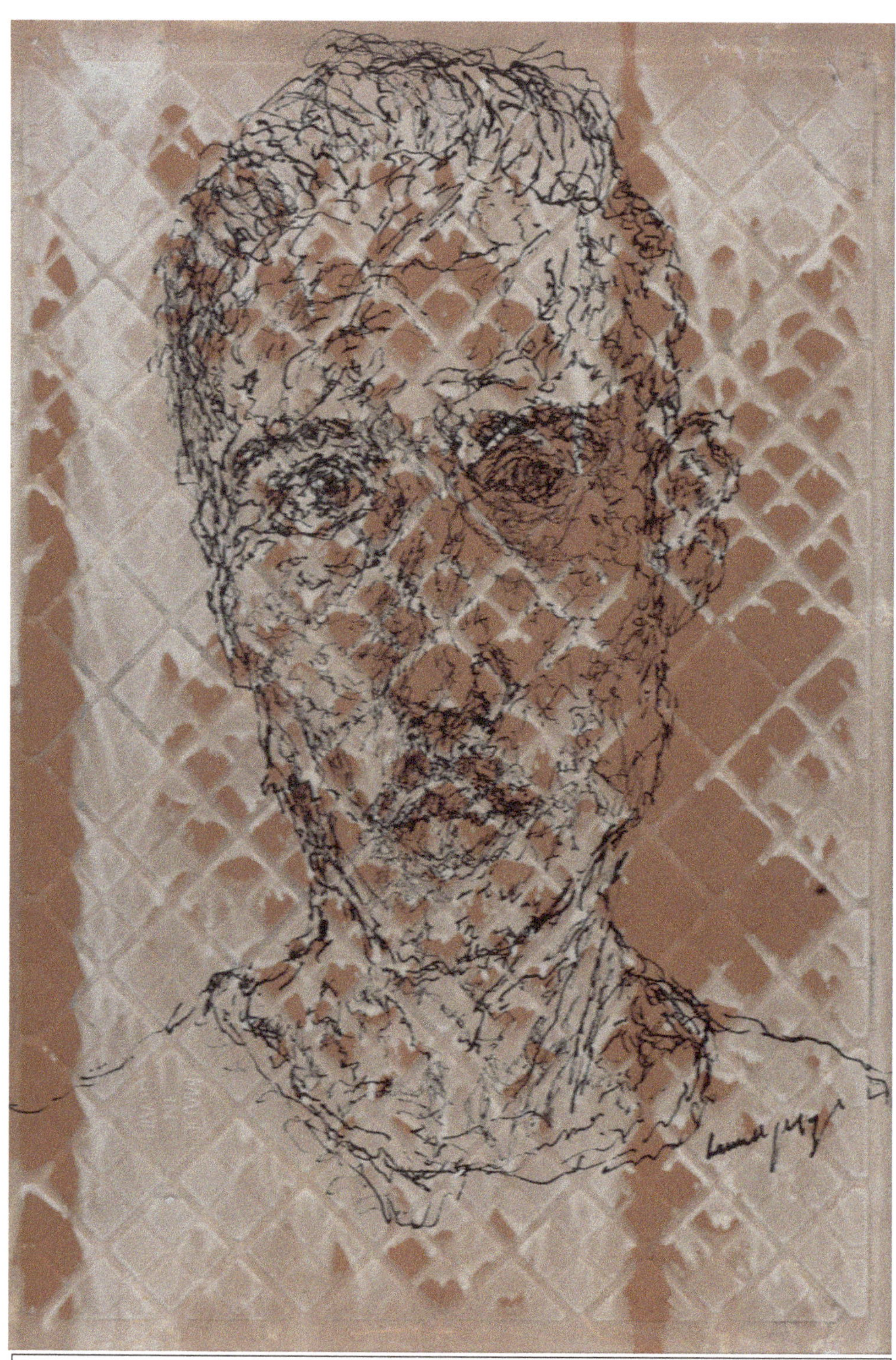

Dan
Ink on the reverse of a recycled tile.
25 x 33.4 cm. 2019.

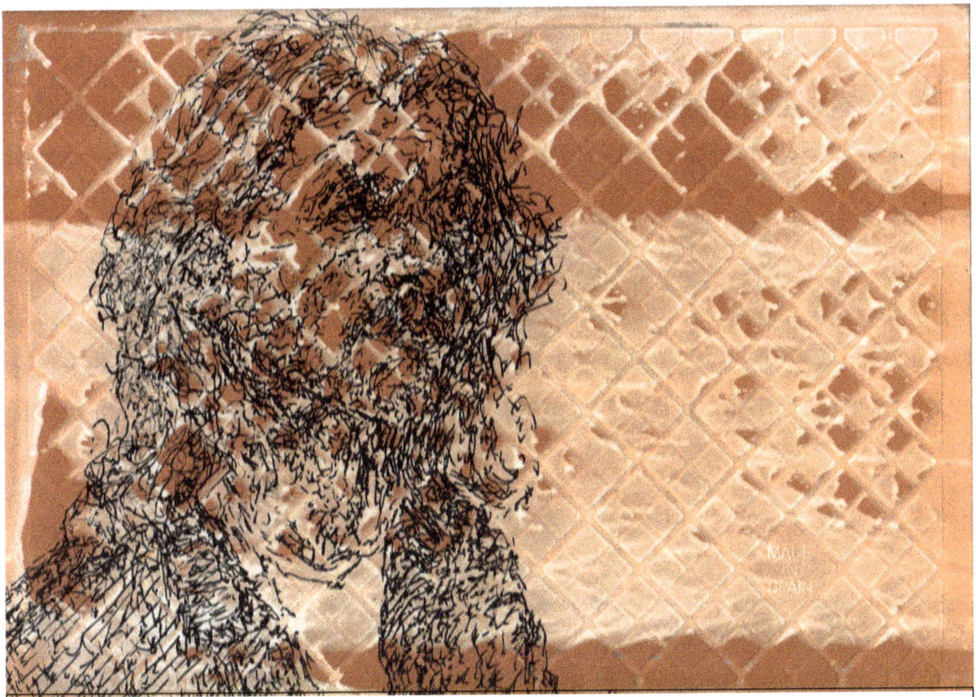

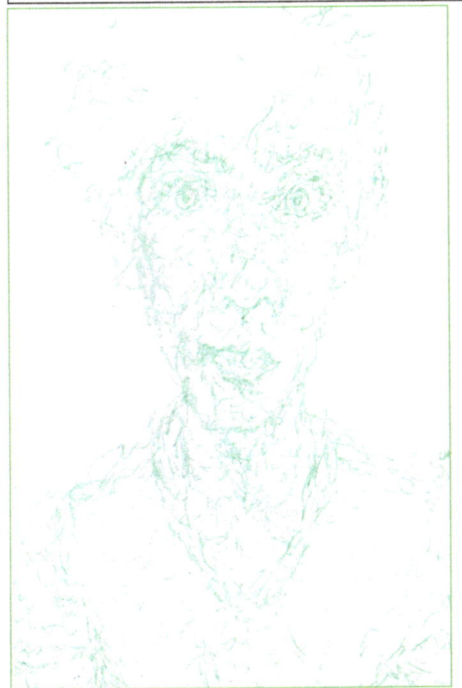

Above:
David Rich
Ink on the reverse of a recycled tile. 33.4 x 25 cm. 2019.
Below:
Postcard Portraits 1 and 2
Ink on card 9 x 14 cm. 2021.

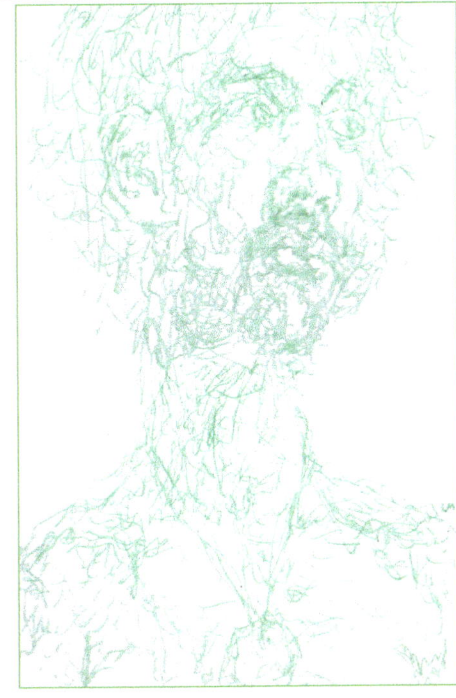

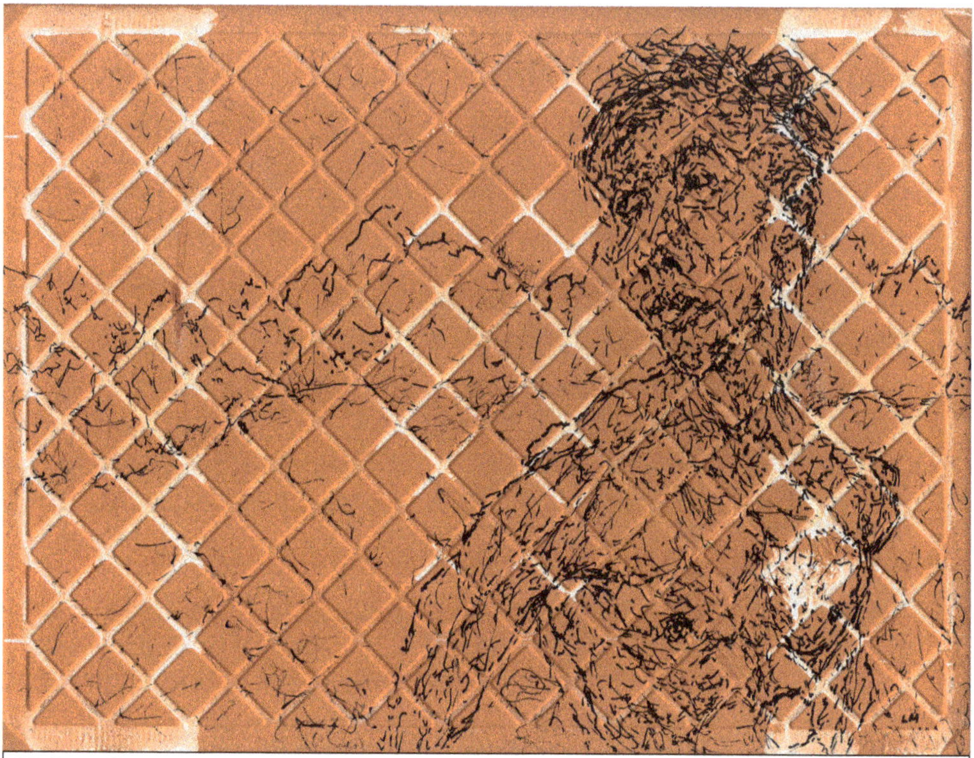

Halong Bay
Ink on the reverse of a recycled tile. 33.4 x 25 cm.

Harry Rich
Ink on the reverse of a recycled tile. 33.4 x 25 cm. 2019.

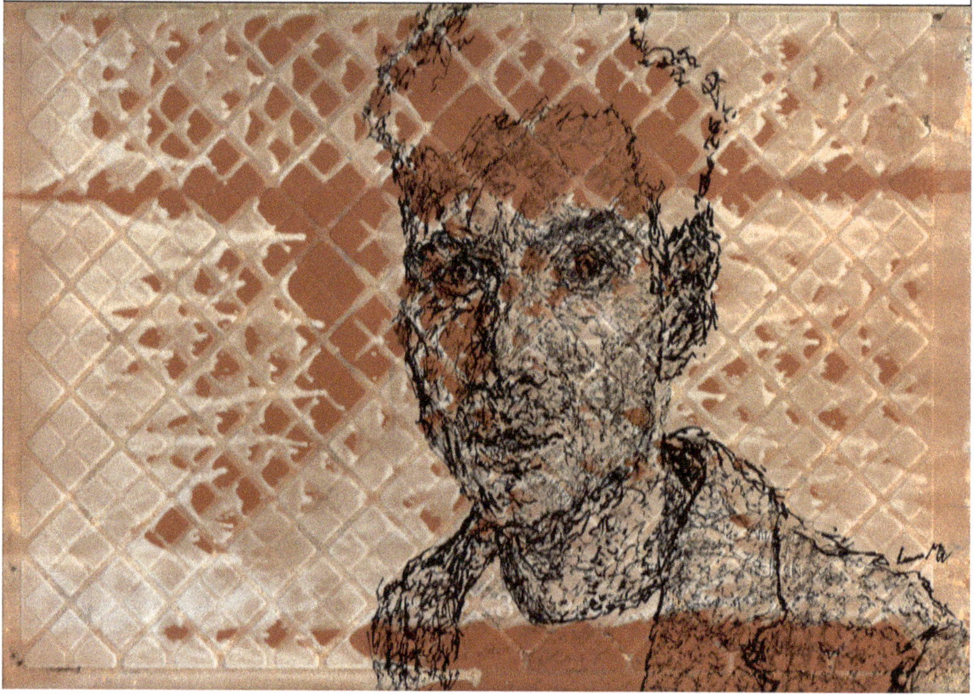

Dorsal
Charcoal on a used jiffy bag.
16.9 x 26.9 cm. 2019.

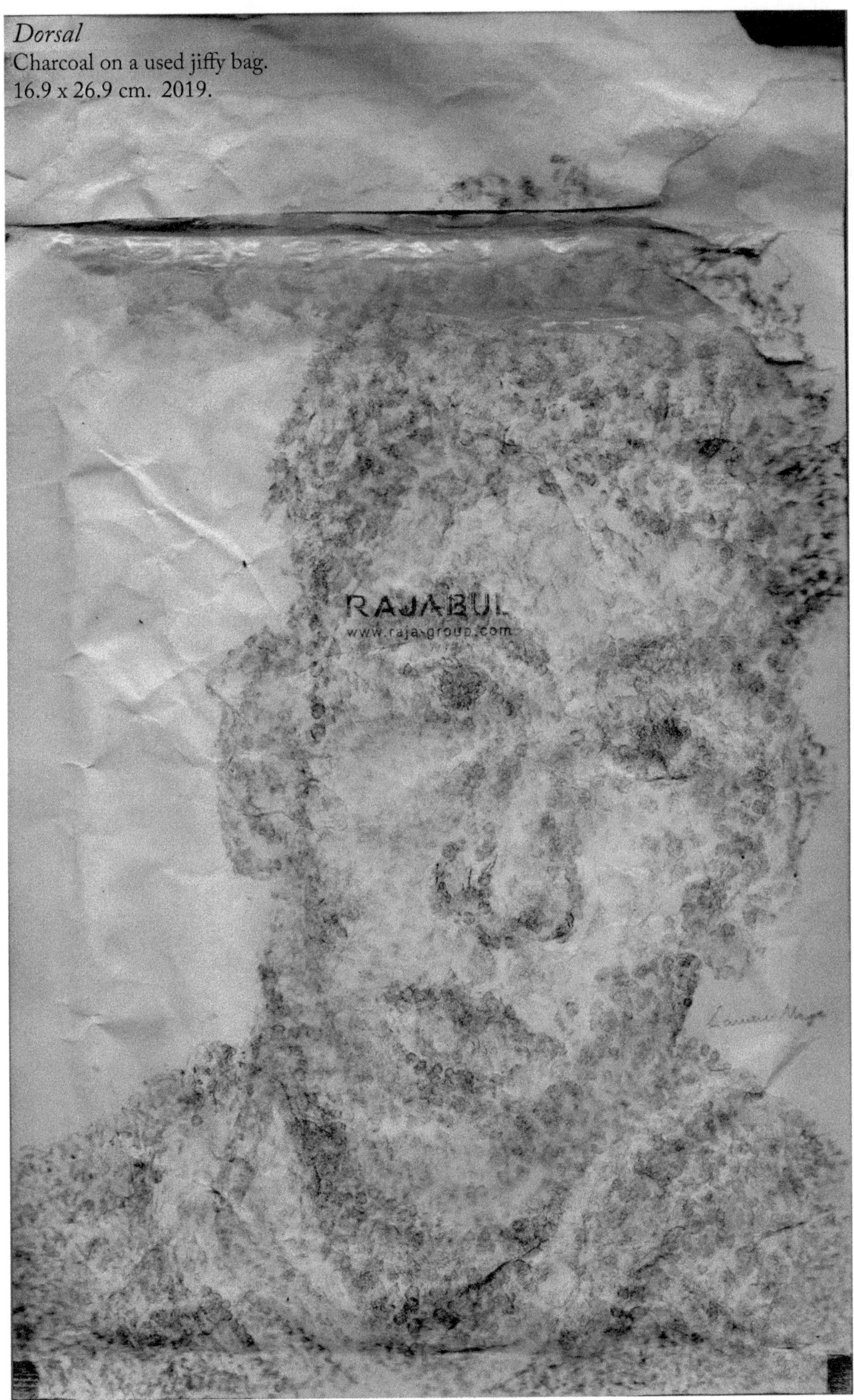

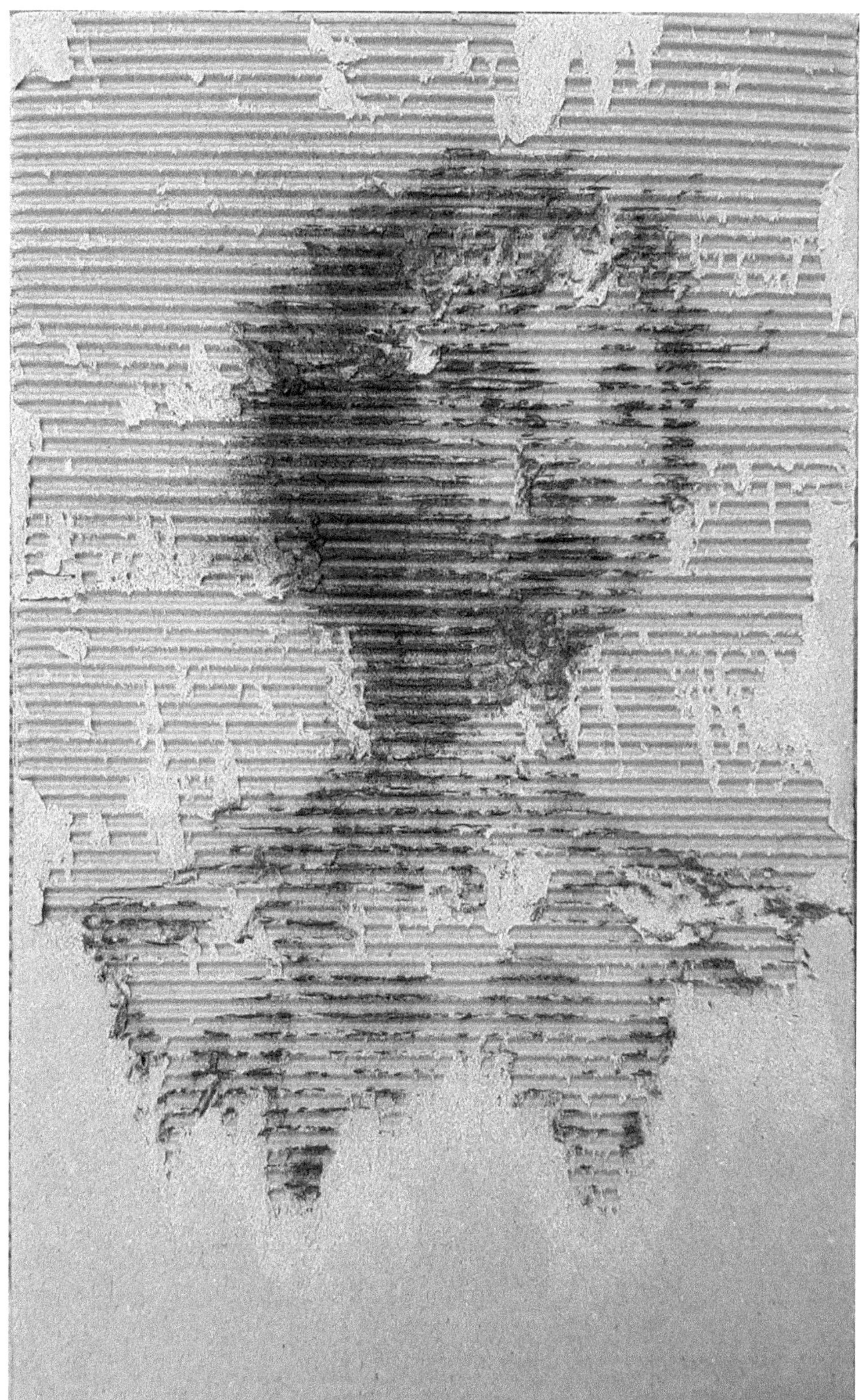

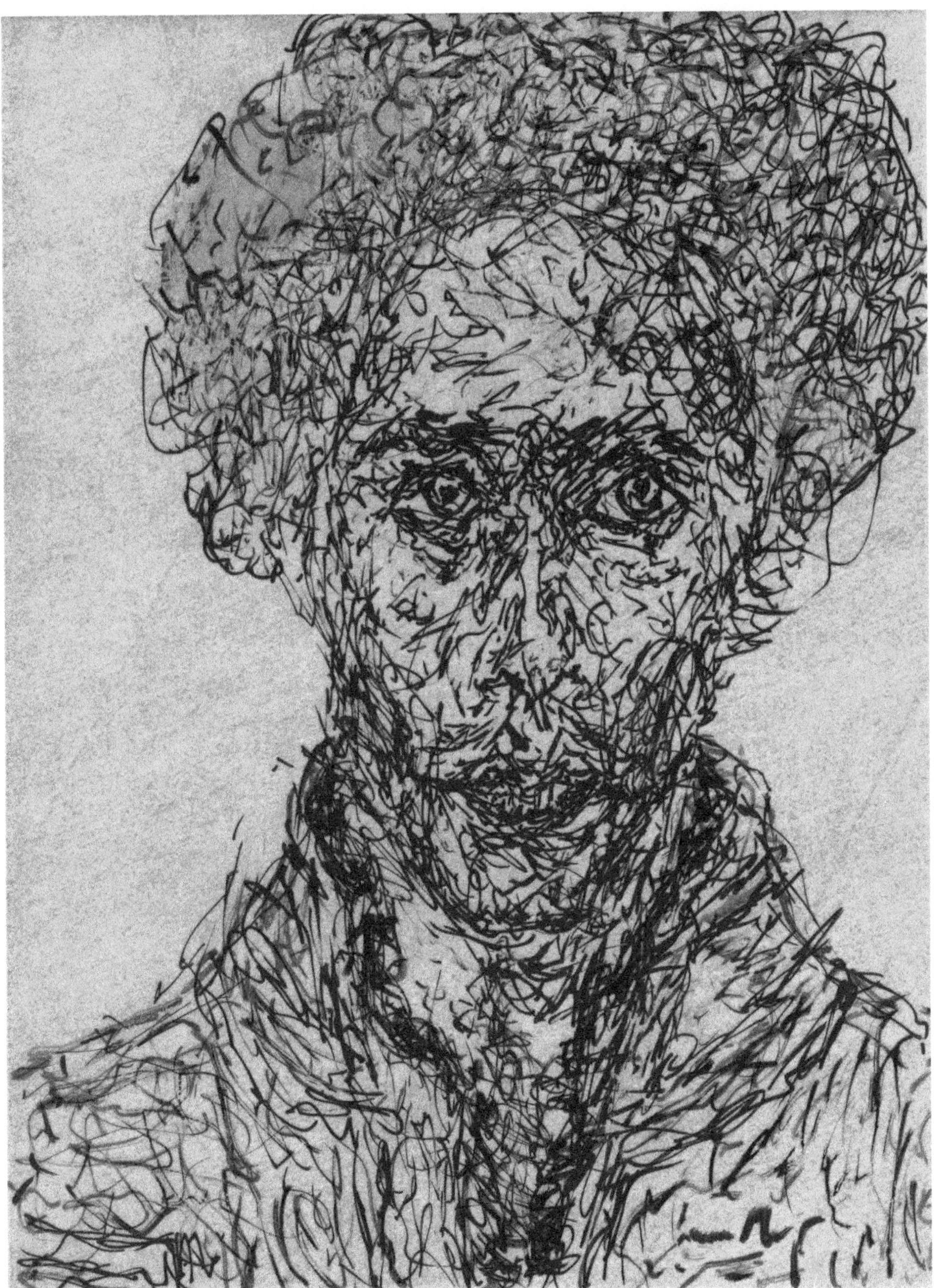

Above:

Just
Ink on tile. 25 x 33.5 cm. 2019.

On page 74 opposite
Tristen
Charcoal on a recycled but intact box. 16.4 x 28.5 (...x 14.5) cm. 2019.

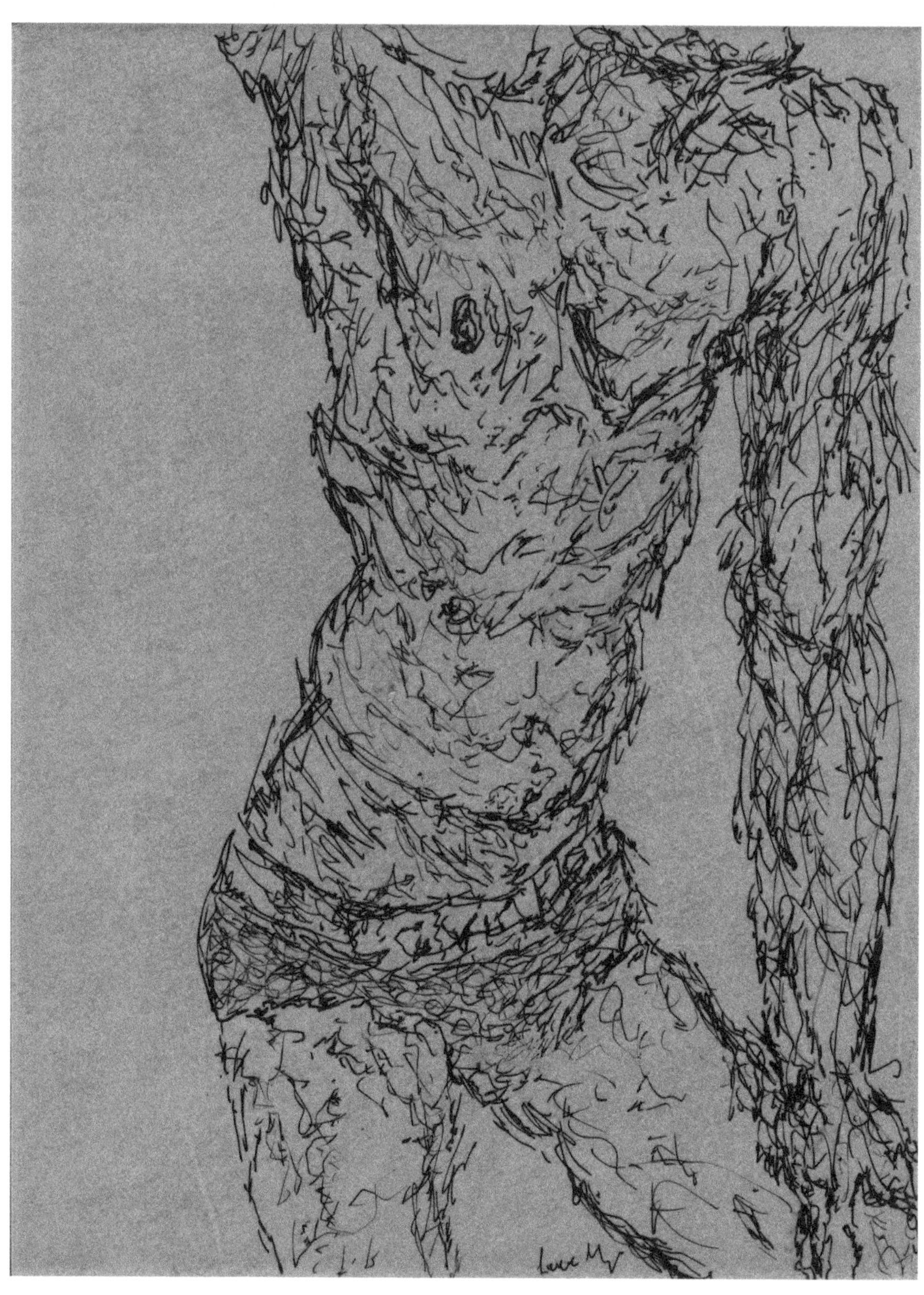

Male Torso 01
Ink on recycled tile.
25 x 33.4 cm. 2020.

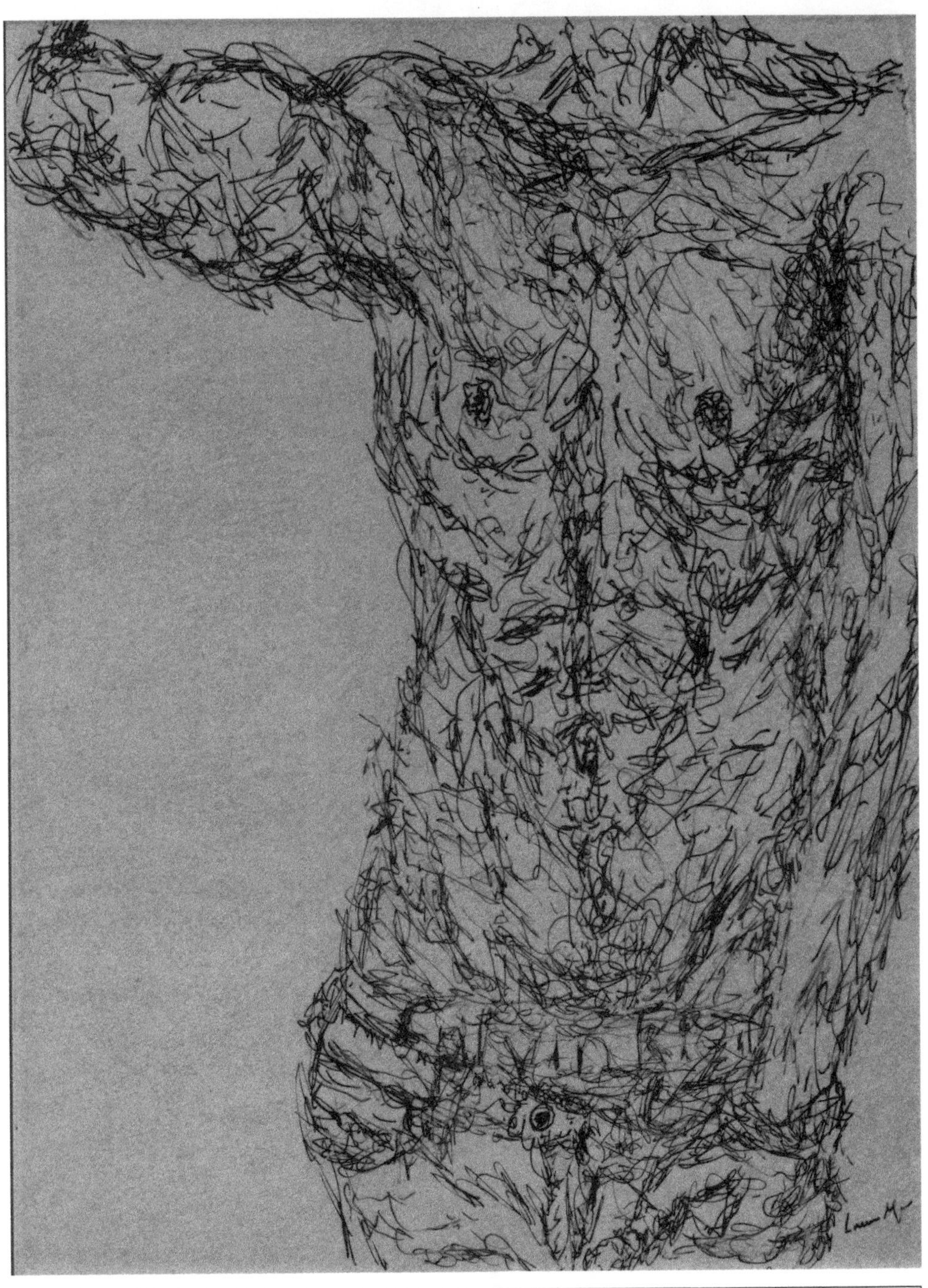

Male Torso 02
Ink on recycled tile.
25 x 33.4 cm. 2020.

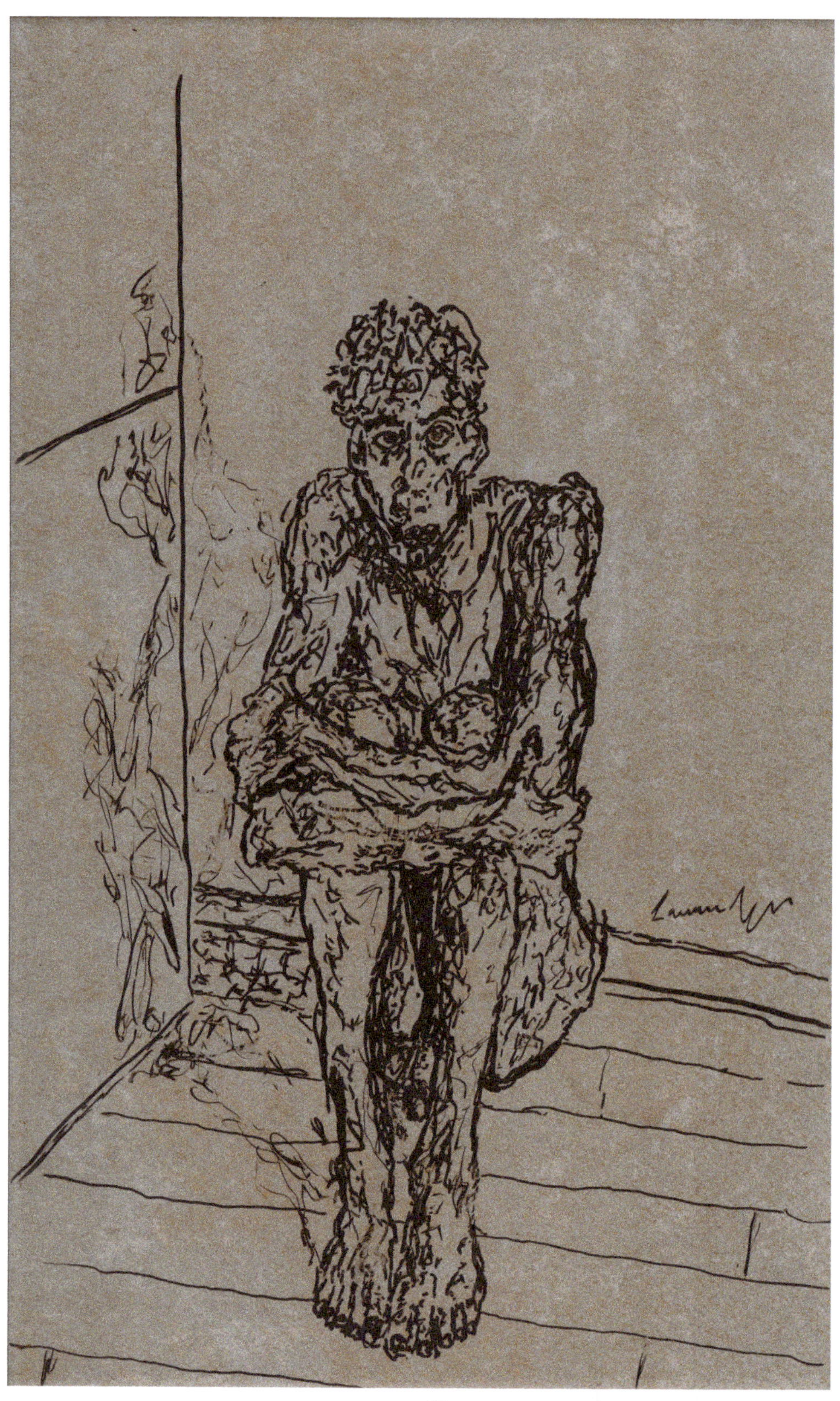

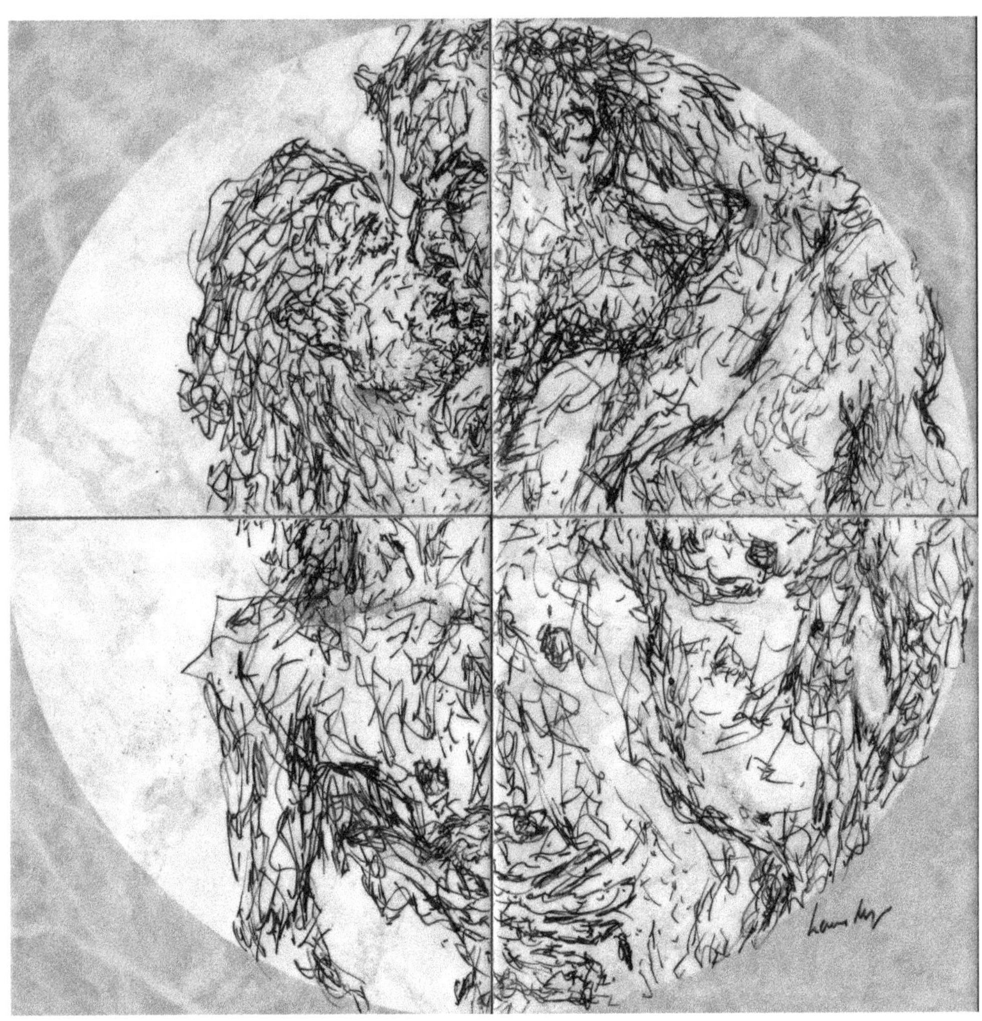

Opposite on page 78

Lime Chilli
Ink on recycled tile.
24.7 x 39.7 cm. 2019.

Above:

Ridges
Ink on recycled tile.
14.6 x 14.6 cm. (17.7 x 17.7 cm. inc. frame) 2017.

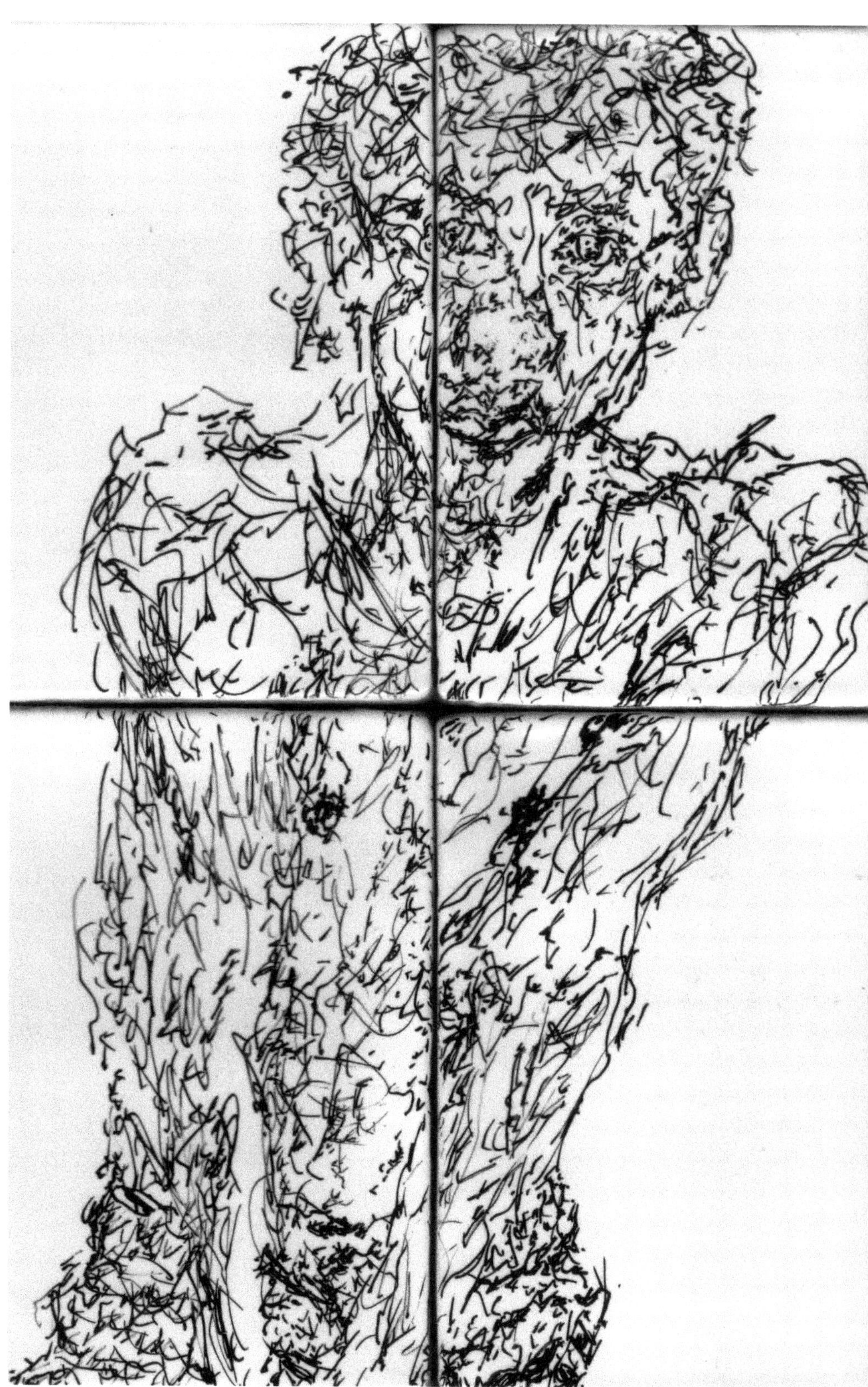

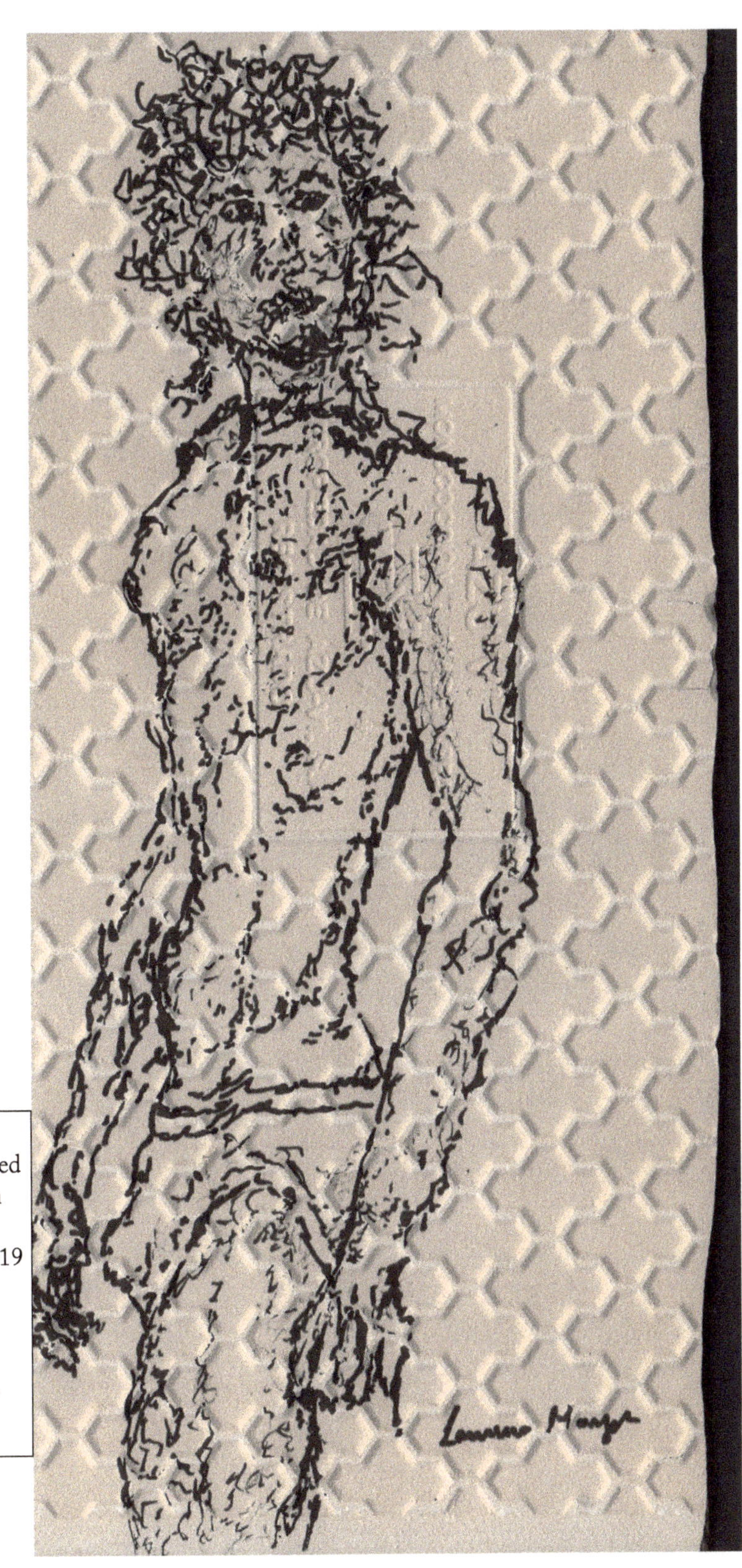

Balaclava
Ink on the patterned
reverse of a broken
tile.
15.7 x 25.4 cm. 2019

On p. 80
Paulo
Ink over four tiles.
26 x 26 cm. 2021.

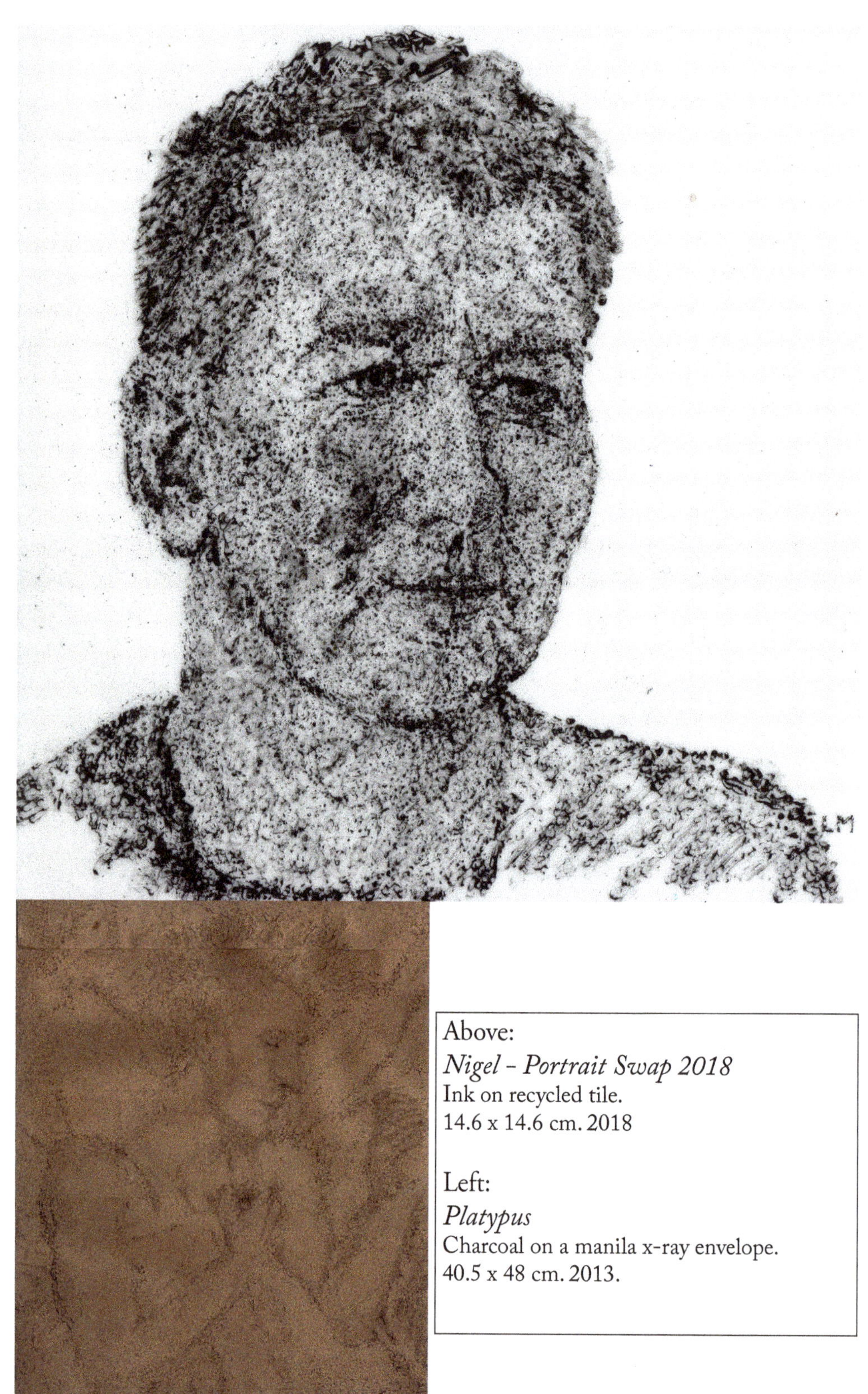

Above:
Nigel – Portrait Swap 2018
Ink on recycled tile.
14.6 x 14.6 cm. 2018

Left:
Platypus
Charcoal on a manila x-ray envelope.
40.5 x 48 cm. 2013.

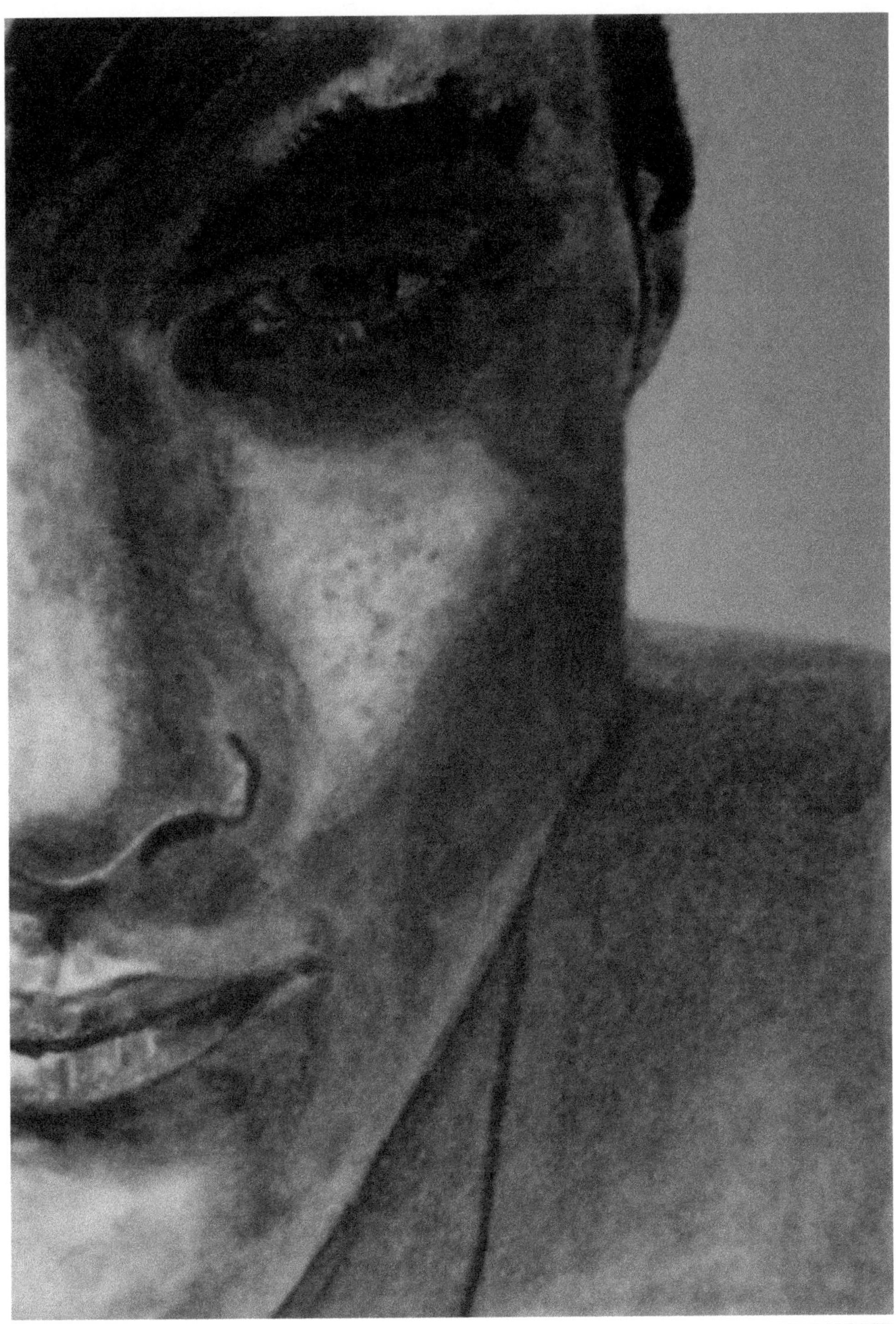

Male 01
Ink on recycled tile.
25 x 33.4 cm. 2020.

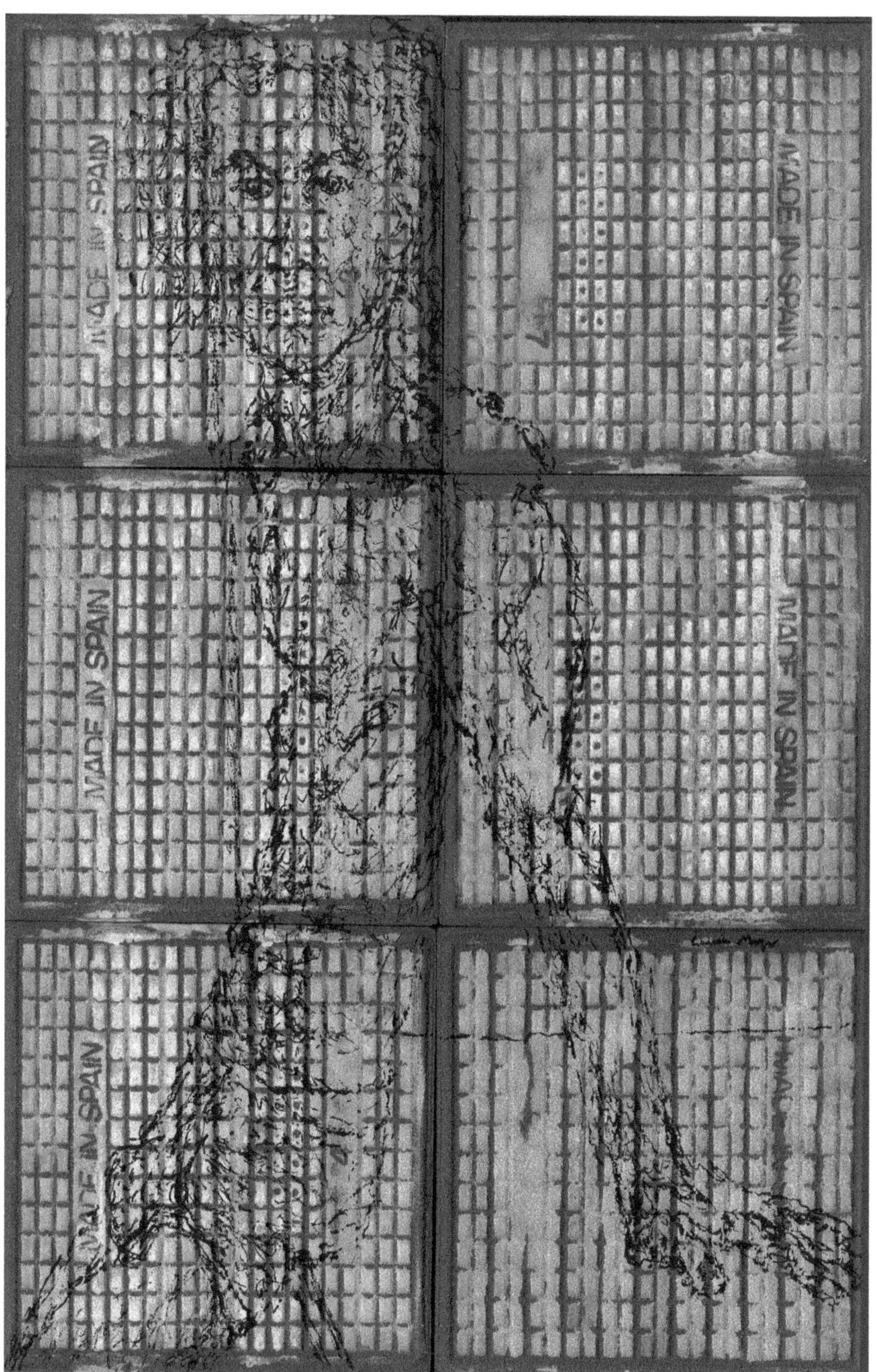

MADE IN SPAIN
MADE IN SPAIN
MADE IN SPAIN
MADE IN SPAIN
MADE IN SPAIN

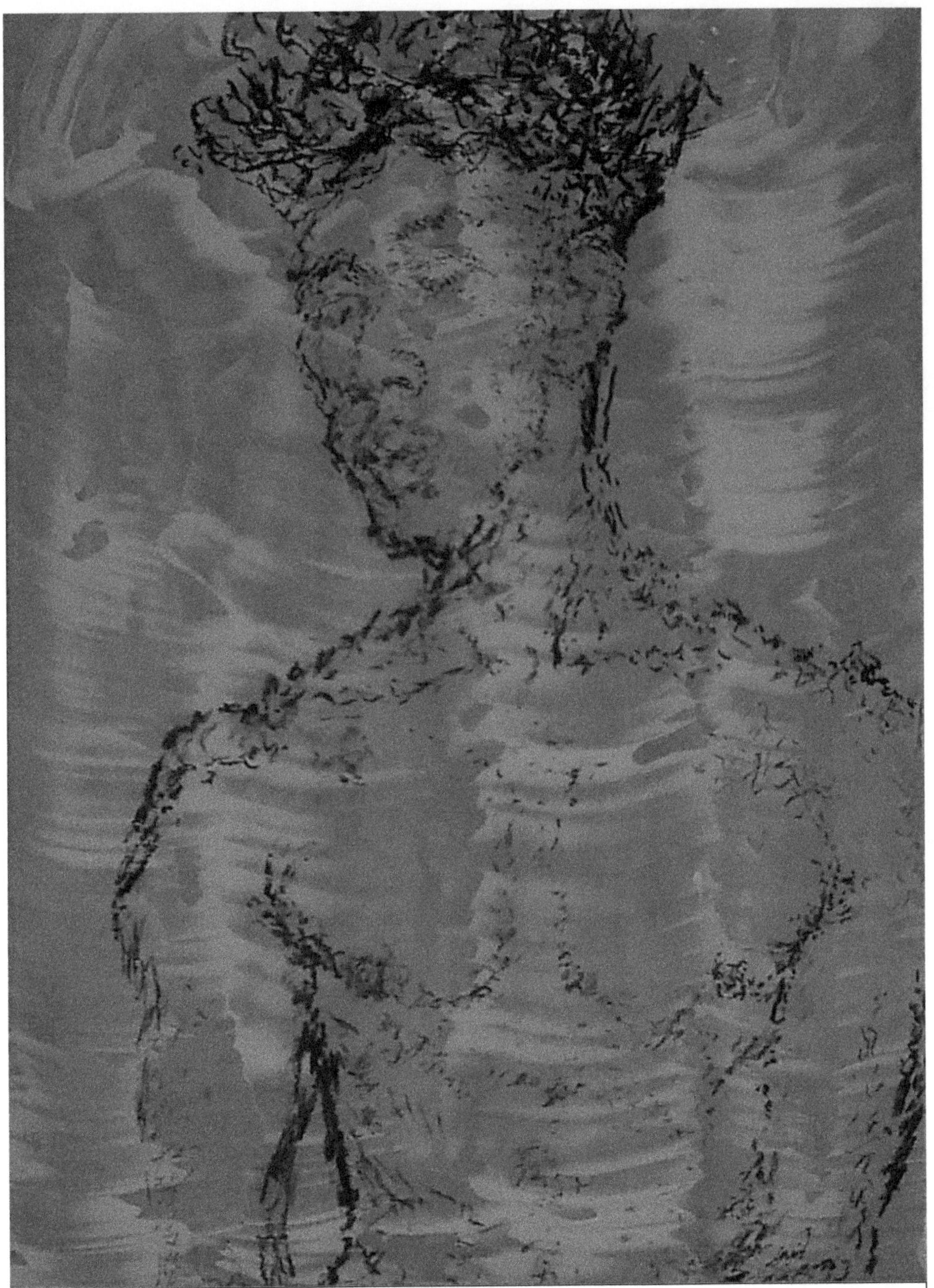

Study Of Jamille
Charcoal on the backboard of a frame, with a loose and partial acrylic white wash. 44 x 62 cm. 2013.

On page 84.

Made In Spain
Ink over the reverse of six recycled tiles. 19.4 x 29.1 cm. 2020

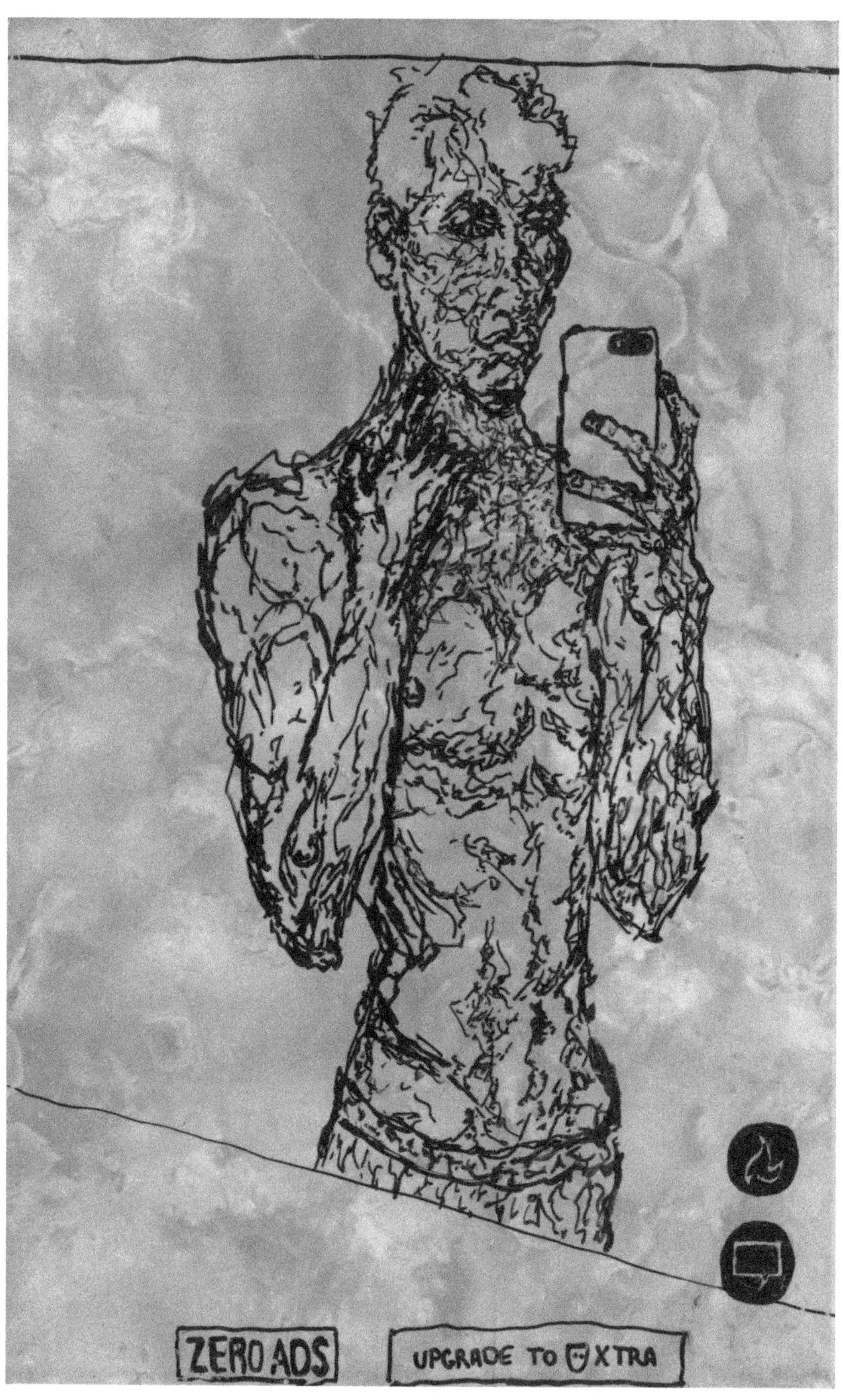

ZERO ADS
UPGRADE TO EXTRA

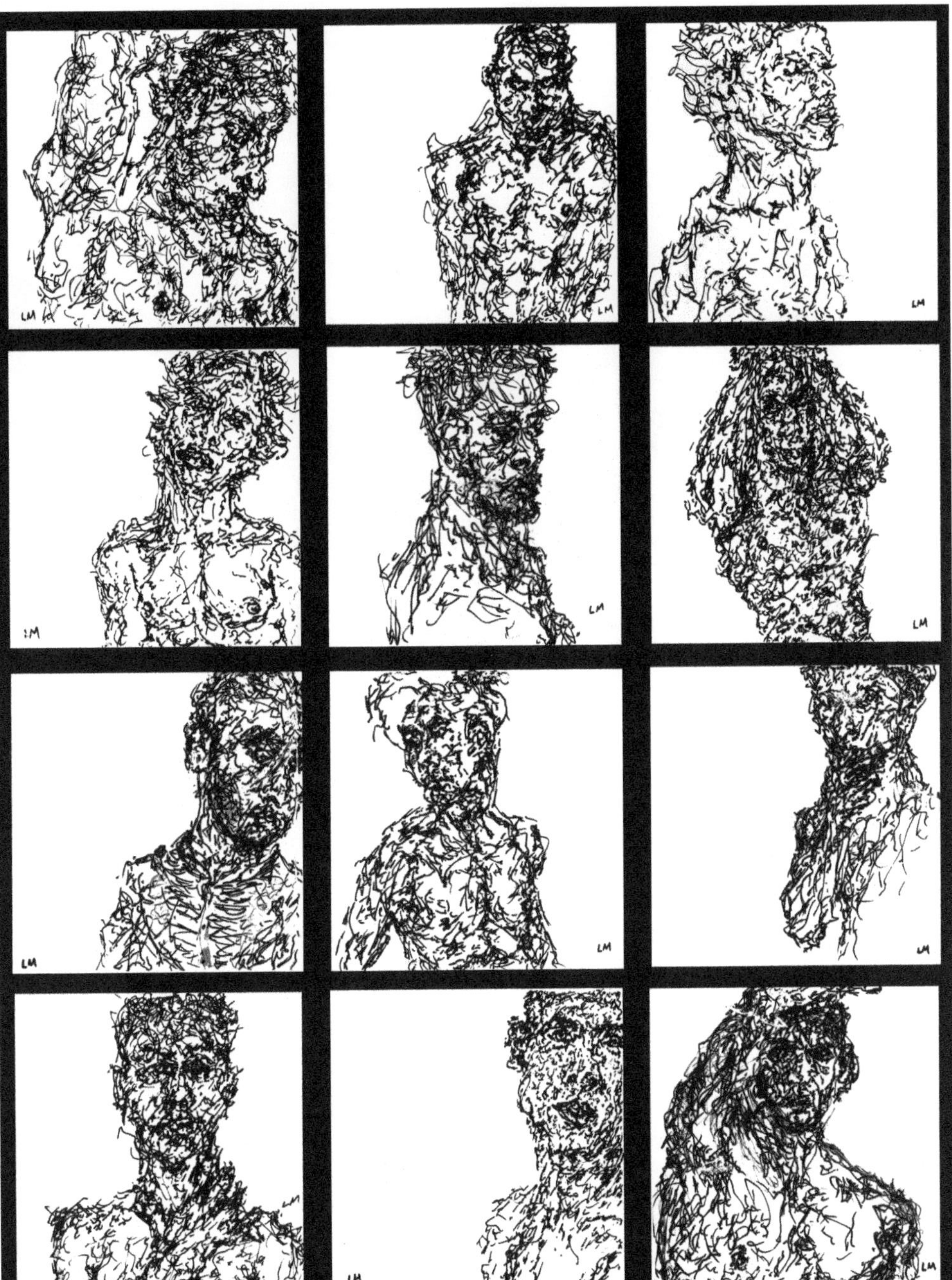

Above:
Sheffield Tiles
Ink on tiles. 13 x 13 cm (individually.) 2020.

Opposite on p. 86
Quick Fix
Ink on tile. 20 x 31.6 cm. 2019.

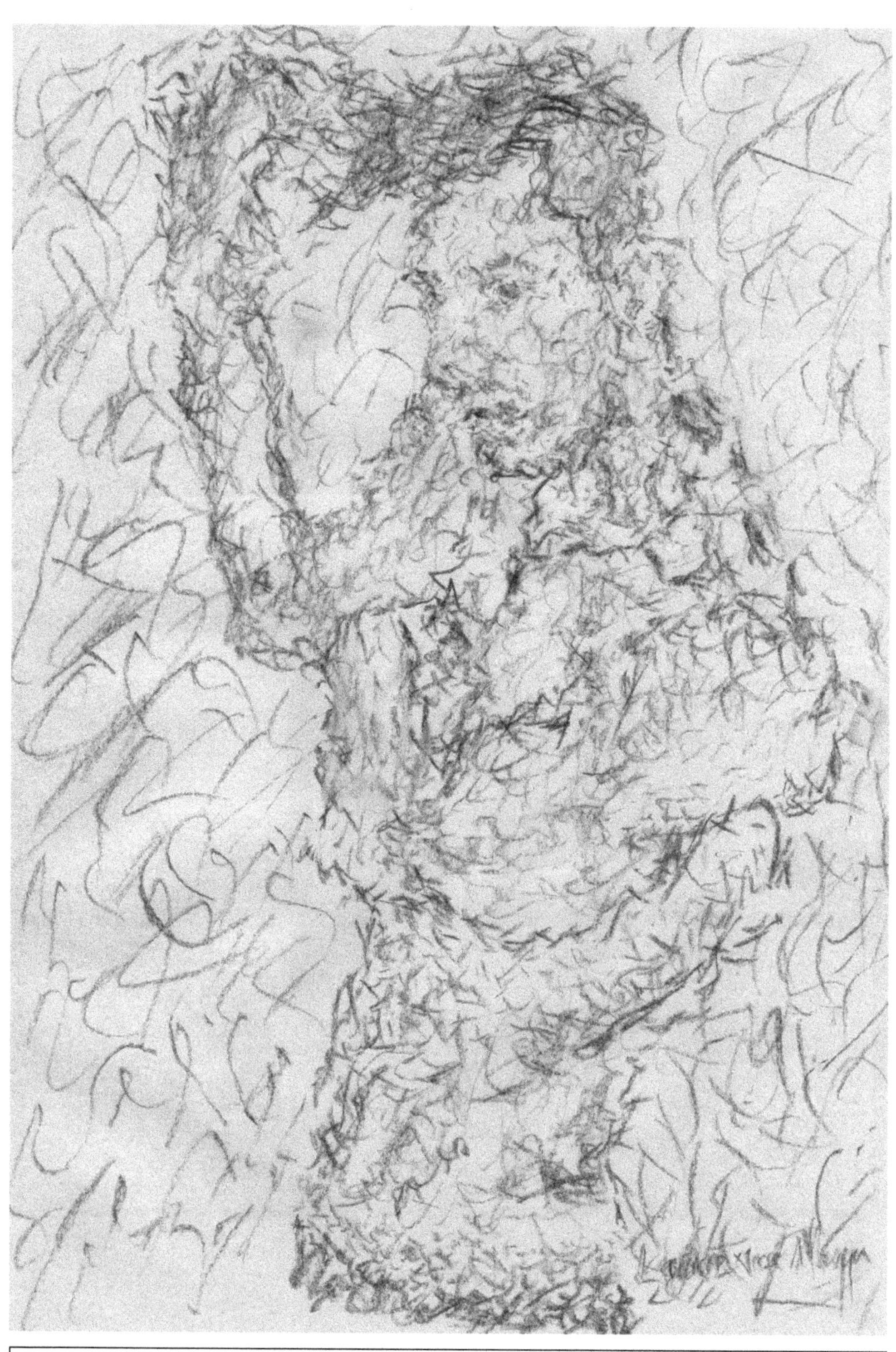

Sawdust
Charcoal on paper.
19 x 27 cm. 2019.

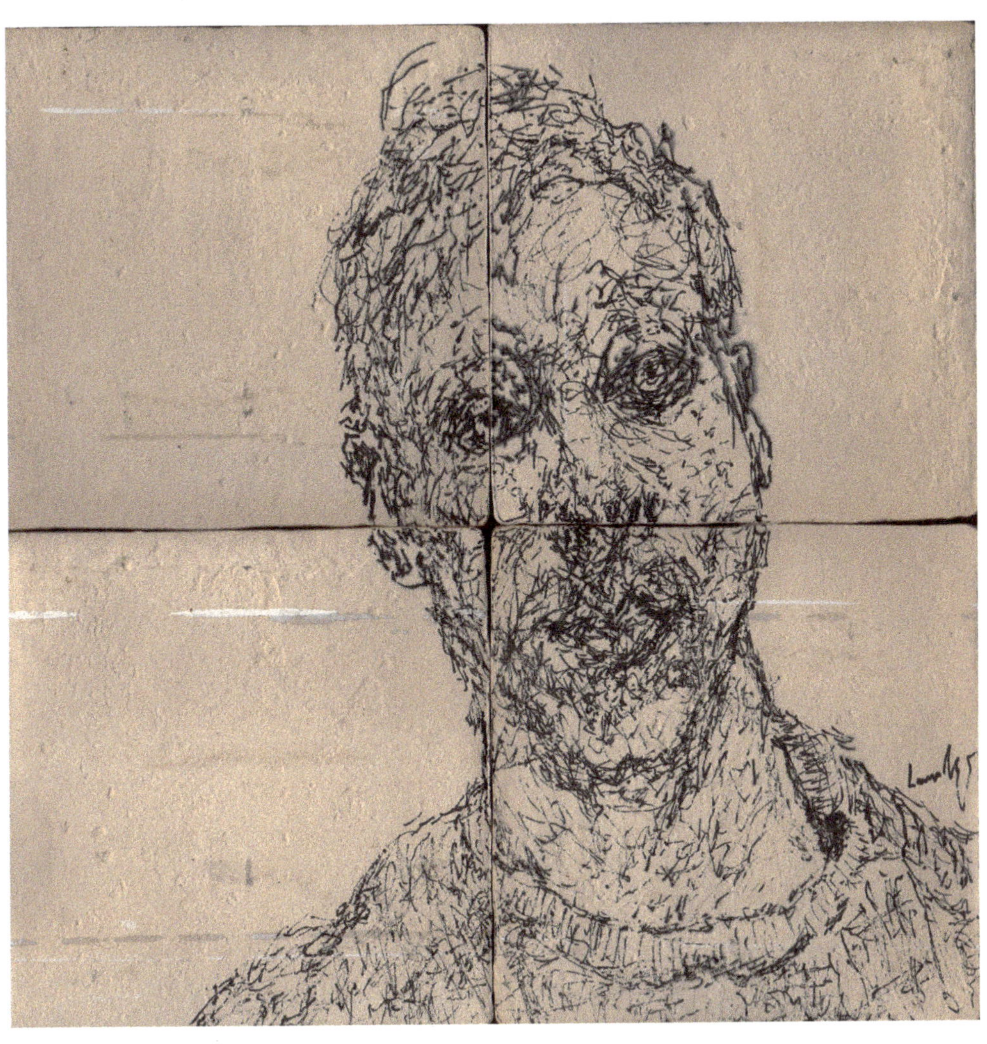

Self Portrait On Reverse Of Tiles
Ink on the reverse of four recycled tiles.
26 x 26 cm. 2021.

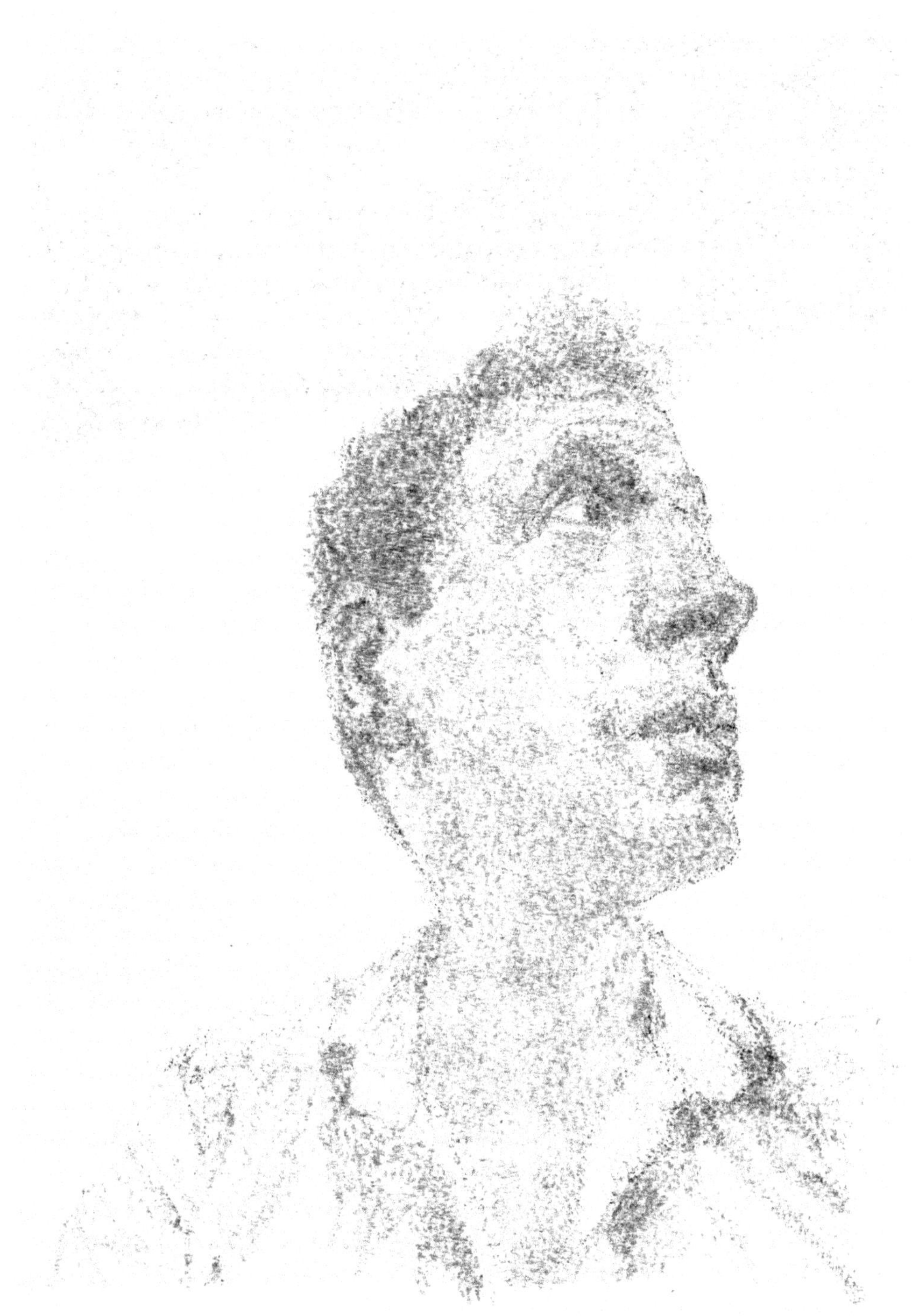

Self Portrait On Paper
Charcoal on paper.
23 x 31.5 cm. 2019.

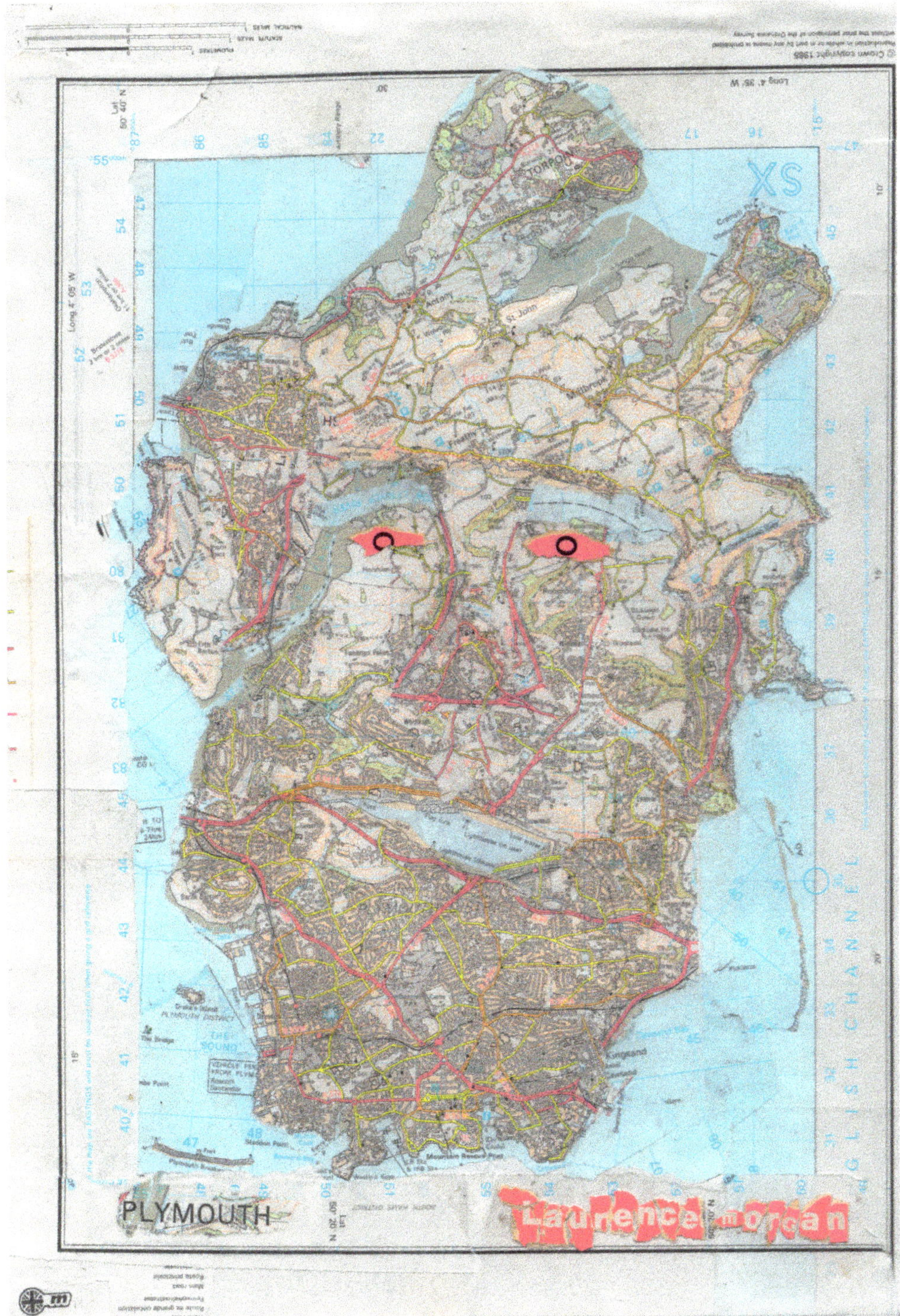

Plymouth
A montage from an OS Landranger map of Plymouth.   30.5 x 40.6 cm. *2021.*
My third of these and the landmass features started to speak to me. A bearded chap started
to come together as I stuck and merged elements.

CPSIA information can be obtained
at www.ICGtesting.com
Printed in the USA
BVHW022313240821
615141BV00016B/369